Offender Rehabilitation Issues

Offender Rehabilitation Issues

Critical Lessons for Criminology, Criminal Justice, and Public Policy

Charles B. A. Ubah

LEXINGTON BOOKS
Lanham • Boulder • New York • London

Published by Lexington Books
An imprint of The Rowman & Littlefield Publishing Group, Inc.
4501 Forbes Boulevard, Suite 200, Lanham, Maryland 20706
www.rowman.com

86-90 Paul Street, London EC2A 4NE

British Library Cataloguing in Publication Information Available

Library of Congress Cataloging-in-Publication Data

Names: Ubah, Charles B. A., author.
Title: Offender rehabilitation issues: critical lessons for criminology, criminal justice, and public policy / Charles B.A. Ubah.
Description: Lanham: Lexington Books, [2023] | Includes bibliographical references and index. | Summary: "This book uses a critical approach to understand the issues and questions about offender rehabilitation within the 21st century"—Provided by publisher.
Identifiers: LCCN 2023021140 (print) | LCCN 2023021141 (ebook) | ISBN 9781666922790 (cloth) | ISBN 9781666922806 (ebook)
Subjects: LCSH: Criminals—Rehabilitation. | Criminal justice, Administration of.
Classification: LCC HV9275 .U23 2023 (print) | LCC HV9275 (ebook) | DDC 364.6/2068—dc23/eng/20230626
LC record available at https://lccn.loc.gov/2023021140
LC ebook record available at https://lccn.loc.gov/2023021141

This book is dedicated to:
My wife and children
Prisca, Priscaflorence, Charlene, Charles II, and William Ubah

Contents

Acknowledgments

With great sense of gratitude, I acknowledge my parents, Theophilus and Florence Ubah, for raising me and my siblings well with lots of unconditional love and affection which helped in many ways for me to be able to produce this book. I hope to love my children the way my dad loved me.

I am deeply grateful to my former professors at the Department of Sociology/Criminology and Criminal Justice at Southern Illinois University at Carbondale, particularly Thomas Burger who more than any other schooled me on how to think critically. I am also grateful to Georgia College & State University for awarding me professional leave which allowed me to devote my time to the research that went into this book. In addition, I benefited from the suggestions and assistance of Antonio Holland, Robert Robinson, Felix Edoho, Obi Ebbe, and Prisca Ubah,

Grateful acknowledgment is also given to the *Prison Journal*; *Journal of Offender Rehabilitation*; *The Pursuit, Journal of Social Science for Policy Implications*; *Justice Policy Journal*; *Journal of Crime, Law, and Society*; and *Journal of Correctional Education* for the opportunity to publish with them some aspects of the material that was reproduced, retooled, updated, and included in this book.

My sincere thanks also go to the entire team of Lexington Books for working closely and diligently with me throughout the publishing processes of this book. Indeed, they are professionals of the first class.

Introduction

Offender rehabilitation is one of the goals of the correctional system and one that virtually all correctional programs and strategies refer to as one of the significant aspects of their objectives. Yet offender rehabilitation remains a very controversial correctional issue that continues to divide scholars, correctional practitioners, policy makers, students, and the public in general (e.g., Denney and Tynes, 2021; Vandala, 2019; Evans, 2018; Austin, 2017; Hall, 2015; Durose et al., 2014; Ubah, 2014; Cullen, 2013; Nally et al., 2012; Taylor and Tewksbury, 2002; Stevens and Ward, 1997; Burton et al., 1993; Martinson, 1974). Some argue that it does work (e.g., Denney and Tynes, 2021; Pelletier and Evans, 2019; Vandala, 2019; Evans, 2018; Fogarty and Giles, 2018: Pompoco et al. 2017; Karpowitz, 2017; Weisburd et al., 2017; Hall, 2015; Ginsberg, 2014; Lewen, 2014; Davis et al., 2013; Kim and Clark, 2013; Steurer et al., 2010; Brazell et al., 2009; Contardo and Tolbert, 2008; Aos et al., 2006b; Batiuk et al., 2005; Jenkins et al., 1995; Porporino and Robinson, 1992; Lockwood, 1991; Anderson 1981; Schumacker et al., 1990), while others think that it doesn't work (e.g., Austin, 2017; Hunt and Dumville, 2016; Durose et al., 2014; Pryor and Thompkins, 2013; Afrifor et al., 2021; Igbo and Ugwuoke, 2003; Sullivan, 1990; Goredki, 1979; Martinson, 1974).

Since prison-based education, especially at the postsecondary level, is a very significant offender rehabilitation program, it is made the focal issue of analysis in this book. Fewer issues in criminology, criminal justice, and public policy are so critical, complex, and controversial as offender rehabilitation issues. Yet, over the years, many offender rehabilitation issues have been examined and analyzed in ways that lack sufficient grounded insights and imagination and fail to be sufficiently probing. For instance, most of the studies on the subject have been mainly concerned with the debate over whether prison-based education works or does not work as measured by the offender recidivism rate (e.g., Denney and Tynes, 2021; Evans, 2018; Karpowitz, 2017; Ubah, 2014; Nally et al., 2012; Matsuyama and Prell, 2010; Anderson, 1981; Cullen et al., 2011; Jenkins et al., 1995; Lattimore et al., 2010; Petersilia, 2004; Porporino and Robinson, 1992; Martinson, 1974), while, to a great degree, they ignored the need to account for other important issues of the programs. Therefore, this book fills the gap. In addition to accounting for the offender recidivism rate of the programs, it also gives adequate attention to other important issues and considerations of the programs, such as academic, employment signaling, institutional function, and social factors. These are important considerations that did not receive adequate attention and scrutiny in the determination of the usefulness or lack of it of the programs. Doing so would enable us to gain deeper insights and imagination of the interacting processes of the programs and glean some important lessons as well as recognize and appreciate the importance of such lessons for criminology, criminal justice, public policy, and the public in general.

Using a critical approach as a tool kit, this book presents important but previously undiscussed or poorly discussed issues and questions about offender rehabilitation and makes adequate efforts to exhaust them; serious lessons were gleaned in the process. This paradigm shift, from the conventional ways this subject is often presented and analyzed is scholarly significant, in that, among other things, it provides broader and deeper insights and lessons that may be too important and too costly to ignore in 21st century criminology, criminal justice, and public policy studies.

The data for this book came from multiple sources of empirical information collected over the decades of this author's study of criminology, criminal justice, and public policy in general and offender rehabilitation programs and recidivism issues as well as their interacting social processes and issues. In addition, what also contributed to the data presented and analyzed in this book is this author's critical and rigorous reviews of much relevant quantitative and qualitative literature on various aspects of offender rehabilitation issues, particularly on prison-based postsecondary education programs.

Offender Rehabilitation Issues: Critical Lessons for Criminology, Criminal Justice, and Public Policy is organized in ways that will enable the reader to gain broader, in-depth, and insightful understanding of the various issues of prison-based postsecondary offender rehabilitation programs, which continue to divide scholars, policy makers, correctional practitioners, students, and the public in general. As such, the issues are too important and too costly to ignore in 21st century criminology, criminal justice, and public policy.

This book is divided into 10 chapters such that the stories told can provoke deeper thinking and imagination on the subject. Chapter 1 highlights the focal issues of offender rehabilitation. It operationalizes the specific aspect of offender rehabilitation the book is particularly concerned about. It highlights the importance of studying offender rehabilitation programs and recidivism issues. The chapter lays the foundation and direction for the rest of the chapters of the book.

Chapter 2 discusses the strengths and weaknesses of individual change perspectives of offender rehabilitation. Among other things, it answers the question of what is it about rehabilitative theoretical perspectives? It identifies and discusses three relevant individual change perspectives of offender rehabilitation, namely, moral development perspective, social-psychological development perspective, and opportunity perspective. These perspectives support the rehabilitative ideal of offender rehabilitation efforts. The chapter also critically analyzes the issues and weaknesses of individual change perspectives of offender rehabilitation and discusses the importance of such issues for criminology, criminal justice, and public policy. In the process of developing this chapter, some important lessons were gleaned, and serious efforts made to exhaust them.

Chapter 3 takes a closer look at the reaction of the pessimistic perspective to individual change perspectives of offender rehabilitation. It identifies, analyzes, and magnifies the issues about individual change perspectives that the pessimistic persuasion reacted to.

Chapter 4 critically examines and analyzes a larger body of empirical evidence on offender rehabilitation correctional education. The empirical evidence on the subject was systematically and rigorously examined beginning before Martinson's 1974 studies of prison-based education programs and the studies published within Martinson's 1974 investigative period, and then those published after Martinson's study periods up to those published recently.

Chapter 5 reaffirms the limits of offender rehabilitation but with caution for criminology, criminal justice, public policy makers, and the public in general. In part or in whole, the cautionary calls the chapter made may be too important and too costly to ignore in any assessment of the usefulness or lack of it of prison-based education programs.

Chapter 6 magnifies the cautions as regards the limits of offender rehabilitation programs and, in the process, gives important warnings and cautionary lessons for criminology, criminal justice, public policy, and the larger public in any determination of the usefulness or lack of it of offender rehabilitation programs. The chapter uses the common conventional approach of recidivism rate measure which most studies on the subject used as the sole indicator of prison-based rehabilitation program usefulness or lack of it to epitomize the cautionary calls it gave. The chapter presents and systematically analyzes other important considerations of prison-based education programs' usefulness beyond their effects on offender recidivism rate. In this chapter, several unique and important lessons can be learned and deeper insights gained.

Chapter 7 presents the history of Pell Grants for prison inmates' postsecondary education programs in the United States, which among other things includes the rationale for the creation of the grants for postsecondary education programs.

Chapter 8 discusses and analyzes the abolition of Pell Grants for higher education of prisoners. In this chapter, you will learn about the political and broader social contexts and processes that contributed to and inform the abolition of Pell Grants for prison inmates' postsecondary education programs and the consequences of the abolition.

Chapter 9 presents and analyzes the eventual end of the abolition of Pell Grants for prison-based postsecondary education programs. In the chapter, you will also learn about social changes and the emergence of new political climates on correctional reform, particularly in the form of the Second Chance Act and the Second Chance Pell Pilot Initiative that partially ended the abolition of Pell monies for prison-based college education programs in the United States, at least for now.

Chapter 10, the last but not the least chapter of the book, presents the limitations of the book and offers plausible directions for future research and draws some conclusions. The strengths of this chapter rest on the lessons and wisdom gleaned from the previous chapters of the book. The chapter reaffirms the distinctiveness of the book as compared to previous manuscripts on the subject.

In keeping within the framework of sociological-criminological imagination approach, this book demonstrates and reaffirms that offender rehabilitation programs and recidivism rates are critical social issues that do not exist in a vacuum but are complex interacting social processes and issues with broader social, economic, legal, and political environmental forces and pressures. As the data presented and analyzed in this book show, the issue of prison-based offender rehabilitation and recidivism rate continues to divide scholars, correctional practitioners, policy makers, students, and the public in general.

The book is unique in some serious respect, in that it approaches the subject of offender rehabilitation and recidivism differently from past examinations. Also, the book critically and systematically raises important but previously undiscussed or poorly discussed issues and questions about prison-based offender rehabilitation, makes adequate efforts to exhaust them, and gleans serious lessons and deeper insights in the process—lessons and insights that might be too important, and too costly to ignore in 21st century criminology, criminal justice, and public policy.

Chapter 1

The Focal Issues of Offender Rehabilitation

THE FOCUS OF THE TEXT

This book is about offender rehabilitation-correctional-education programs, which are very critical and complex issues in criminology, criminal justice, and public policy. Unlike Martinson's (1974) study, which examined the generality of offender rehabilitation programs on corrections in general, this book focuses specifically on the prison-based postsecondary education program, which is a very significant aspect of the offender rehabilitation and reintegration process. To be clear, prison-based postsecondary education opportunities include programs such as career/technical program certificates, associate degrees, bachelor's degrees, and even graduate degrees, for inmates who have a GED or high school diploma (Duwe, 2018). The reasons why the book focuses on postsecondary correctional education programming rather than GED programs are:

A. This author thinks that if any correctional education programming would have the propensity to impact offenders generally and thus lead to a significant reduction in recidivism, college-level educational programming is probably the most likely. As Ubah (2002:18) succinctly instructs, "Education should not be viewed as some uniform and homogenous entity exposure to which gives skills and alters thinking and motivation invariably in the same fashion." In part, this is because the credentials and skills inmate might acquire by participating in prison-based postsecondary education programs can increase their human capital (resources that increase saleable abilities in people such as marketable skills and trades) much more than GED programs would.

These necessary human capital resources can help some inmate to "go straight" and abandon the life of crime when released from a correctional institution into the general society.

A. This thinking is informed and supported by a growing body of research; for example, Sweetland (1996) argues that college-level correctional educational credentials, rather than a GED, can open up better job opportunities for ex-offenders, which in turn can build social bonds that protect against criminal behavior. Tootoonchi (1990) asserts that college education programs offered in correctional institutions are intended to redirect inmates' attitudes, talents, and energy toward a more constructive and meaningful purpose in the future (also see, for example, Denney and Tynes, 2021).
B. This author is interested in investigating the possible impact of prison-based Pell Grants elimination, which concerns only college-level correctional-educational programming.
C. Participation in GED courses is mandatory in almost all penal institutions across

American; thus, there is no nonparticipating comparison group that would allow an estimate of education's impact on offenders that participated in the programs.

Why Should We Study Offender Rehabilitation Issues?

The study of offender rehabilitation issues is important for various reasons especially for criminology, criminal justice, and public policy. The reasons include, but are not limited to, the fact that offender rehabilitation is one of the goals of the correctional system and one that virtually all correctional programs and strategies referred to as one of the significant aspects of their objectives. Yet offender rehabilitation remains a very controversial correctional goal that continues to divide scholars, correctional practitioners, policy makers, students, and the larger public (e.g., Denney and Tynes, 2021; Vandala, 2019; Evans, 2018; Austin, 2017; Hall, 2015; Durose et al., 2014; Ubah, 2014; Cullen, 2013; Nally et al., 2012; Taylor and Tewksbury, 2002; Stevens and Ward, 1997; Burton et al., 1993; Martinson, 1974). And since prison-based education, especially at the postsecondary level, is a very significant offender rehabilitative program, it is made the focus of this book (e.g., Evans, 2018; Kim and Aos et al, 2006b). Offender recidivism rate is often used as the sole indictor of prison-based education program usefulness or lack of it while ignoring other important considerations (e,g., Duwe, 2018; Ubah, 2005; Wilson et al., 2000; Martinson, 1994). This book, therefore, fills the gap by making sure that in addition to giving adequate attention to the offender recidivism rate consideration aspect of the subject, adequate attention is also given to other important considerations of the subject beyond its recidivism rate value such as academic, political, economic, social, signaling, and institutional function values of the subject.

This sociological-criminology imagination approach utilized in analyzing identified relevant interacting social processes and forces of offender rehabilitation issues is a paradigm shift from the conventional ways the subject was often examined previously. Therefore this book is scholastically significant, in that, among other things, it will enable us to have broader and deeper insights and understanding of the academic debate over prison-based education programs and offender recidivism. It will provide broader and deeper insights and lessons that may be too important and too costly to ignore for corrections policy and practice. It will help policy makers to have broader and deeper understanding of the interacting processes and factors at work so they are able to make critical and informed decisions about whether the programs should continue to exist and, if so, how they can be structured and funded (e.g., Denney and Tynes, 2021; Muhlhausen and Hurwitz, 2019). It will help send signals to employers as they make employment decisions on whether to hire an ex-offender or not (e.g., Vandala, 2019; Gaes, 2008). And it will shed deeper and broader insights on some of the social issues concerning prison-based education programs and causes of offender recidivism (e.g., Denney and Tynes, 2021; Evans, 2018; Kim and Clark, 2013). Therefore, this book provides broader and deeper insights and lessons that may be too important and too costly to ignore in 21st century criminology, criminal justice, and public policy.

For instance, Mandel (1963:2) states that:

> Without the studies on recidivism, it is impossible to compare the efficacy of correctional programs among correctional agencies and institutions. With the studies it becomes feasible to focus attention upon those programs which appear to have the greatest salutary effects upon the offenders whom they reach.

In line with Mandel's insightful suggestions, Robinson (1990) articulates what the author of this book thinks encompasses very good suggestions of the potential policy implications of the recidivism rate considerations value of studying prison-based education programs and offender recidivism rates. Robinson stresses that studies on offender recidivism rates will aid policy makers and correctional administrators in making critical decisions about whether rehabilitative programs should continue to exist and, if so, how they should be structured, administered, and funded; they will aid policy makers and correctional administrators in identifying effective and viable rehabilitative programs; and they will enable them to focus attention upon the programs that appear to have the greatest efficacy upon the offenders they serve. Studies of these programs may also assist correctional administrators in identifying variables that serve as predictors of inmate success in the programs and predictors of successful program utilization.

As the debate over prison-based education continued to divide scholars, correctional practitioners, policy makers, and the public in general, this book adds to that debate by rigorously and critically examining the usefulness or lack of it of prison-based education programs from the perspective of broader considerations of its other important values beyond merely its significant rate of recidivism reduction measure. As a result, the book instructs future studies on the subject to utilize multiple criteria in any determination of the usefulness or lack of it of the programs and not only with recidivism rate measurement. Unlike most studies on the subject, the book provides deeper insights and lessons of the academic, political, economic, social, employment signaling, and institutional functions importance of prison-based college education programs beyond their effects on offender recidivism rate and the recognition and appreciation of the importance of the insights and lessons for the understanding of prisons in particular, criminology, criminal justice, and public policy in general.

SUMMARY

Overall, most of the studies on the subject are mainly concerned with the debate over whether prison-based education programs work or do not work, as measured by offender recidivism rate, while to a great degree they ignored the need to give adequate attention to other important considerations such as academic, political, economic, social, employment signaling, and institutional values. In this book an explicit and compelling case is made for the other important considerations of prison-based education programs beyond their impacts on recidivism rate. In the process, some valuable lessons are learned and deeper insights gained, and the importance of such lessons and insights for criminology, criminal justice, and public policy are recognized.

Chapter 2

Individual Change Perspectives of Offender Rehabilitation

It is important to begin this chapter by first addressing the question of what is a theory? In doing so, it will not only enable us to set a solid foundation for the main subject matter of the book but will also enable us to conceptualize, explain, predict, and understand the subject matter much better. Simply put, a theory consists of a collection of an interrelated, organized, and systematic set of ideas that describe an unobserved aspect of the world (e.g., Lilly et al., 2010; Ward and Maruna, 2007; Williams and McShane, 2014). Thus, Ward and Maruna (2007:32) postulate nicely what a theory really is:

> Theories are used both to explain and predict phenomena. Explanation is basically the application of a theory to help understand certain phenomena and is backward-looking (i.e., helps understand why a particular outcome happened). By contrast, prediction is forward-looking and is concerned with the forecasting of outcomes within a person, group, institution, or physical system.

The question, then, is what is it about offender rehabilitation theory? Offender rehabilitation theory is supposed to guide research on offender rehabilitation. It should aid in part or in whole in the explanation of the phenomenon of offender rehabilitation. It should be an explanation of how the process is supposed to work (e.g., Simon, 1993). It should ask the question of "how it works," which in turn leads to the determination of "what works and what doesn't in reducing offender recidivism rates (e.g., Latessa et al., 2015; Lin, 2000; Martinson, 1974).

In effect, offender rehabilitation perspectives such as individual change approaches (moral-development perspective, social psychological development perspective, and opportunity perspective) presented and analyzed in this book should attempt to explain prison-based education programs as mechanisms for offender rehabilitation and reintegration from prison into the general society. But the perspectives might not necessarily account for the full truth of both why inmates exposed to such programs had a certain outcome and what exactly are possible with the programs as much as other theoretical perspectives and/or approaches might. Ward and Maruna (2007:31) put it succinctly: "We accept that even our best theories may only be partially true and that it is possible that for any given scientific problem there could be more than one way of solving it."

Considering this well-established fact, this treatise does not in any way claim to contain a complete account of a theory of rehabilitation nor does it pretend to account for the full truth of the phenomena under examination. Instead, it takes a grounded and closer look at some individual change perspectives on prison-based education rehabilitation programs and makes serious efforts to articulate a narrative of some of them for consideration in the efforts to explain and understand offender rehabilitation issues.

WHAT IS IT ABOUT INDIVIDUAL CHANGE PERSPECTIVES OF OFFENDER REHABILITATION?

Prison inmate rehabilitation is one of the goals of the correctional system. But is inmate rehabilitation possible? If so, how, and if not, why not? There is a body of perspectives that are based on the notion that a degree of inmate rehabilitation and reintegration can be achieved through prison-based education programs, that is, that inmates' exposure to such education program is a contributing cause of lowered recidivism and productive citizenship (e.g., Denney and Tynes, 2021; Vandala, 2019; Ubah and Ubah, 2019; Evans, 2018; Fogarty and Giles, 2018; Drake and Fumia, 2017; Linden, 2015; Ubah, 2014; Davis et al., 2013; Lilly et al., 2010; Ward and Maruna, 2007; Williams and McShane, 2010).

These perspectives can be sociologically, psychologically, and economically deterministic in nature. The perspectives, collectively, can be referred to as "individual change perspectives." Individual change perspectives include but are not limited to moral-development perspective, social-psychological development perspective, and opportunity perspective (e.g., Vandala, 2019; Ubah and Ubah, 2019; Ubah and Robinson, 2002). Individual change perspectives can also be referred to as idealistic/optimistic rehabilitation perspectives (Ubah and Ubah, 2019). Therefore, these two conceptual frameworks (individual change perspectives and idealistic/optimistic rehabilitation perspectives) are used interchangeably in articulating the three perspectives that are the focal analytical approaches utilized in this book. Thus, perspectives of individual change focus directly on the individual offender as the point of analysis and only indirectly on the larger society (Ubah and Robinson, 2002).

The question, then, is what is it about individual change perspectives of offender rehabilitation? Central to individual change perspectives of offender rehabilitation as articulated by penologists, criminologists, sociologists, educators, and public figures is an assumption that correctional education programs can enhance the successful reintegration of some individual inmates from the society of captives into the general society (e.g., Denney and Tynes, 2021; Vandala, 2019; Linden, 2015; Bui and Morash, 2010; Bushway and Apel, 2012; Hipp et al., 2010; Wang et al., 2010; Cullen, 2007; Ubah and Robinson, 2002; Sykes, 1958). In other words, these perspectives can be referred to collectively, as "perspectives of individual change" (Ubah, 2014; Ubah and Robinson, 2002). Perspectives of individual change focus directly on the individual offender as the point of analysis and only indirectly on the larger society.

Based on these perspectives, the questions, therefore, are what is it about rehabilitation theory and what is it about the prison-based education program that reduces offender recidivism—is it its building of moral character, self-esteem, and self-concept? Is it its provision of a new perspective on life, with attendant reorientation of action; its function as a coping mechanism; the know-how it provides; new interests; its function as a credential in the labor market? The theoretical perspectives of individual change of offender rehabilitation and related issues and approaches that will be explored here address some of these questions (e.g., Ubah and Ubah, 2019; Ward and Maruna, 2007; Ubah and Robinson, 2002). We may begin with moral-development perspective.

Moral-Development Perspective

As Ubah and Ubah (2019) reaffirmed, moral-development perspective is a perspective of individual change that is very optimistic about the potential of correctional rehabilitative programs. The perspective hypothesizes that prison-based education programs that offer liberal-arts classes such as philosophy, sociology, history, or literature can be rehabilitative in their effect because these courses seem to strengthen people's conscience as they confront the moral and ethical dilemmas addressed in the study of liberal arts (e.g., Denney and Tynes, 2021; Vinney, 2019; Szifris, 2017: Latessa, 2012; Ward and Maruna, 2007; Peterson and Seligman, 2004; Ubah and Robinson, 2002: Jablecki, 2000; Lockwood, 1991; Arbuthnot and Gordon, 1986; Duguid, 1981).

This perspective is based on the assumption that role-taking opportunities are crucial to producing positive movement in people's morality and behavior through the various stages of cognitive-moral development processes. It predicts that role-taking leads to empathy—the awareness of others as having thoughts, feelings, and needs like once's self (Denney and Tynes, 2021; Ubah and Ubah, 2019; Colvin, 2016; Latessa, 2012; Lockwood, 1991). The ground-breaking ideas of this approach originated from the work of Max Weber, which can be traced to his concept of *verstehen*—a Germany word meaning "to understand" (Parsons, 1968) and brilliantly reformulated and popularized by George Herbert Mead, as discussed in his influential book *Mind, Self, and Society: From the Standpoint of a Social Behaviorist* (Mead, 1934; Morris, 1962). Mead provided a model of how interaction processes are the basis of moral development in humans. Perhaps his model can best be captured in the belief that individuals are the product of society and social interaction.

Although, the perspective originated from the work of Weber and was greatly reformulated and popularized by Mead, however Herbert Blumer's ideas on the subject are profoundly significant in this discussion and, as such, deserve to be referenced at least briefly. Thus, Blumer suggested that individuals act toward things based on the personal meanings that the things have for them and that the meanings of things arise out of social interaction and are handled and modified through an interpretative process, thus coining the term "symbolic interactionism" to describe the perspective (Blumer, 1969; Ubah and Ubah, 2019).

It is because of the power of Weber's, Mead's, and Blumer's brilliant ideas of the perspective, as well as other distinctive authors such as Garfinkel, Cooley, Goffman, Best, and Berger, that courses that are believed to improve role-taking abilities are often recommended as central components of correctional education programming (Evans, 2018; Szifris, 2017; Colvin, 2016; Ubah, 2003; Jablecki, 2000; Hobler, 1999; Fabiano, 1991; Rose, 1985; Samenow, 1991). However, it is important to note that the values of such programs in the transformative process of offenders' experience are not uniform across gender and some other social groupings and perhaps may have more to do with the meaning offenders give to the programs, their self-perception of personal roles/statuses and the things they encounter in the process (Evans, 2018; Vandala, 2019; Szifris, 2017: Latessa, 2012; Herrschaft et al., 2009).

Nevertheless, research has demonstrated that moral reasoning programs can produce transformative attitudinal change in individuals such inmates in various degrees and forms and some of those can be very significant in their effect (e.g., Denney and Tynes, 2021; Vandala, 2019; Colvin, 2016; Wilson, 2011; Brewster, 2010; Hobler, 1999; Lockwood, 1991). For instance, Hobler (1999) postulates that moral education can enable individuals to look at themselves in different ways and to begin to make decisions based upon moral reasoning (such as in Lawrence Kohlberg's conventional stage of moral development) rather than self-satisfaction (such as in Lawrence Kohlberg's pre-conventional stage of moral development) (e.g., Vinney,

2019). Such insights suggest that if we teach inmates to think in a rational, moralistic mode, it will follow that their behavior and actions would probably adjust appropriately (e.g., Denney and Tynes, 2021; Ubah and Robinson, 2002). Perhaps, this possibility is what Evans (2019:4) who participated in the prison-based education program known as Common Good Atlanta (CGA) and Hello World, meant when he articulated his experience and those of his fellow participants in the programs in his essay "The Elevating Connection of Higher Education in Prison: An Incarcerated Student's Perspective" that:

> In my first few years of incarceration, I felt like inventory on a dusty shelf in a warehouse. Looking at my life from that shelf, I was merely "on hold" until I got out. This induces a lot of self-pity. However, once I immersed myself in education programs for creative writing, liberal arts, and computer programming, I no longer saw it that way. I still have a life, even in prison, and I am learning and growing, not just occupying space. CGA and Hello World pulled me out of a cave of false beliefs and a warehouse of stagnation by providing me opportunities to stimulate my intellect and immerse myself in constructive projects—like writing essays and computer programs—that increase my knowledge and understanding as well as productively occupy my time. My expanded empathy for others and consciousness about the world has also helped me exit that cave and warehouse because my world is no longer just about my problems. The more wrapped up I am in my own issues, the more apathetic I become, which leads to a lack of concern about how my words and actions will impact others. When I focus on other people and their struggles, I am far more likely to consider how what I do or say will affect them.

Jablecki (2000), in his work "Prison Inmates Meet Socrates," observed the power of such liberating processes by articulating that inmates of Texas Department of Corrections (TDCJ) exposed to educational programs fashioned upon Socrates's teachings especially on his concepts of "unexamined life is not worth living" and his "identification of knowledge and virtue" experienced profound positive changes in their thinking and conduct and consequently reduced their recidivism rates by enhancing their successful reintegration into the general society. Thus, Jablecki's (2000:3–4) suggestions of the positive changes in the thinking and conduct of the inmates in the Texas program can be captured in the following findings:

> The students find that courses in history, literature, and philosophy profoundly deepen their sensitivities and expand their horizons. TDCJ students may come from pockets of economic and intellectual poverty from which they have never escaped—they have literally no knowledge of other ways of living. Humanities courses open new realities to them, wholly changing their perspectives about who they are and what the world is about. . . . Such courses are truly revelations, showing ways of living and thinking that they have not encountered before.

The significance of this transformative process of human skill, which is centered on "empathy," clearly extends far beyond its value in the offender rehabilitative process in prison but also has connections with other social settings and is relevant and highly needed in our ever-increasing technological world. The truth of that can be captured succinctly in the brilliant work of Colvin (2016) titled *Humans Are Underrated: What High Achievers Know That Brilliant Machines Never Will* in which he describes empathy as "the critical 21st-century skill" employers are desperate for more so than any other skills when making employment decisions. To epitomize this observation, Colvin (2016:73) states that one high-level executive at a software company, Oracle, described empathy as "the skill I need to develop in myself, my team, and my children" and concludes that "empathy will be the difference between good and great."

Contrary to Goffman's (1961) suggestion that once an individual is tainted it is impossible to regain normalcy unless that person's stigma could be hidden. Evans (2018) and Jablecki (2000), on the other hand, suggest otherwise considering their findings. Their findings are particularly relevant to the issue of identity transformation (see, for example, Vandala, 2019; Veysey, 2008; Ebaugh, 1988; Goffman, 1961) and the evaluative aspect of the offender rehabilitation process which entails the development of the ability to reexamine self and begin to make better practical judgments, and to formulate and implement life plans that embody socially acceptable values (Vandala, 2019; Ward and Maruna (2007). Thus, Ebaugh (1988) and Veysey (2008) seem to support Evans and Jablecki's suggestions by arguing that role exit is possible and could take the process of realization and dissatisfaction with the current role, consideration of available alternative roles, gradually modeling a new role and transition into the new role (see also Latessa, 2012). Hence, Herrschaft et al., (2009) put it well when they assert that one catalyst of a change process can begin a cascade of changes. These transformative processes in the offender rehabilitation effort in part or in whole are in line with the premise of moral development theory as supported by a growing body of research.

By the same token with the above assertions, Ward and Maruna (2007:36) seemed to capture the profound relevance of the resources of moral and ethical values in the offender rehabilitation process by asserting that "ethical values are a particularly important set of resources as they represent foundational, or core standards used to construct ways of living and behaving. They bestow a sense of meaning, significance and purpose on human lives and are at the heart of the rehabilitation process." Arguing within the framework of this perspective, Duguid (1992) stresses that if there is such a dimension of latent human development and growth in us all, perhaps more than anything else, education becomes a potential key, a means of identifying, liberating, and exploring that humanness. Concurring with Duguid's views, Johnson (1964:610) asserts that "the school is viewed as a cure-all for social problems. . . . 'Good parenthood' and high moral values are supposed to come from classroom experience. Since education deals with the development and change of human behavior, the faith in education as a treatment tool is well placed."

As interesting and insightful as this perspective might seem, some issues remain unaddressed or poorly addressed and some of those issues will be examined and addressed more so after we look at the other two individual change perspectives we are focusing on in this text. On that note we now turn to social-psychological development perspective.

Social-Psychological Development Perspective

Another perspective of individual change that can be used to justify correctional rehabilitative programs is social-psychological development perspective (e.g., Vandala, 2021; Ubah and Ubah, 2019; Ubah and Robinson, 2002). The perspective emphasizes the potentially transformative and liberating processes set in motion by educative experiences. The perspective suggests that social cognitive processes play a prominent role in the acquisition and retention of new behavior patterns. It rests on the general assumption that cognitive shifts—new behavioral patterns can be elicited in an individual through exposure to certain modes of treatment such as correctional education programming (i.e., academic and vocational) (e.g., Ubah and Ubah, 2019; Vandala, 2021; Evans, 2018; Link and Williams, 2017; Crabtree at el, 2016; Colvin, 2016; Linden, 2015; Ward and Maruna, 2007; Ward and Stewart, 2003; Jablecki, 2000; Orpinas et al., 1996).

Social psychological development perspective has been described as a personality perspective (e.g., Veysey, 2008). A personality perspective draws on an empirical research base which suggests that personality noncriminogenic constructs (such as low self-control, poor self-esteem, personal distress, and interpersonal distrust) are necessary contributing factors in the process of antisocial behavior both within and outside the prison walls (Evans, 2018; Latessa et al., 2015; Andrews et al., 2006; Ogloff and Davis, 2004). Hence, Mears and Mestre (2012) assert that because of the values of such constructs they should be considered in a holistic offender desistence process.

In "Rethinking Reentry," Veysey (2008:4) makes an insightful observation that "treating addiction, symptoms of a mental illness, or criminogenic needs will have limited success when the person receiving treatment perceives other things to be the primary problems." According to Veysey, this is because what led people into criminality is not necessarily the pathway out in reverse. Ward and Maruna (2007:102) underscore Veysey's observation by asserting that there is utility in targeting noncriminogenic needs in a therapeutic process because:

> Focusing only on the reduction of criminogenic needs may reduce risk, but without inculcating other methods to achieve goals risk is likely to reemerge. . . . In other words, attending to features of individuals' lives such as personal distress or the interpersonal manifestation of low self-esteem is a mandatory not a discretionary aspect of effective therapy.

Thus, the premise of social psychological development perspective rests in part on the promise that certain prison-based offender rehabilitation programs would help alleviate the individual's crime supportive attitudes, values, beliefs, and emotions and consequently lead to desistence from criminal behavior and potentially resulting in lowered recidivism rates (Latessa, 2012; Wormith et al., 2007; Andrews and Bonta, 2003).

Theorists using this approach to correctional education programs are of the view that inmates' completion of or participation in education in prison will enhance their psychological well-being through their development of cognitive and physical abilities that could enable them to relax better than before, release tension more maturely, express themselves more constructively, and build self-esteem and a favorable self-concept that can help them work toward a crime-free future (e.g., Ubah and Ubah, 2019; Evans, 2018; Brennan, 2012; Mears and Mestre, 2012; Karstedt, 2008; Ubah and Robinson, 2002).

By the same token, Ubah and Robinson (2002:117–18) postulate that "according to the theory, correctional education would make prisoners feel more human, make prison more bearable by limiting the effects of some of its degradation, and foster the prisoner's health and safety because he or she has more mental and physical stimulation than previously." In addition, it would enable them to cope more maturely than before and be more able to envision and signal a replacement of a criminal self and identity to prosocial self and roles (Evans, 2018; Bushway and Apel, 2012). On that note, Hackman (1997:74) asserts that:

> Education is an opportunity for an improved lifestyle. An inmate who has been locked up with no opportunity for self-improvement could be released with pent up anger and a "society owes me" attitude. This, in turn could start the cycle of crime spinning again. However, through education, those who did not realize they have the capacity to succeed or improve their life with a saleable skill could be released from prison with a positive attitude and become a productive member of society. Education is an opportunity to turn a negative experience (incarceration) into a positive experience (rehabilitation).

If Hackman's assertion is correct, inmates' participation in prison-based education programs becomes a way to cope maturely and constructively with the complex difficulties of prisonization, dehumanization, and contracted life of prison-based correctional institutions (Evans, 2018; Delisi and Conis, 2019, 2013; Ubah and Ubah, 2019; Welch, 2004; Irwin, 1985; Clemmer, 1958; Garfinkel, 1956). When this happens, time spent in prison can be viewed as a constructive painful experience (Evans, 2018). All these potentials of correctional education programs suggest that inmates earning a college degree tend to look at the world more positively, set higher standards and goals for themselves, and learn to manage their time better (e.g., Denney and Tynes, 2021; Vandala, 2019; Pendleton, 1988). On the contrary, without correctional education programs, inmates are left to their own limited resources and all-defeating criminogenic imagination and tendencies (e.g., Delisi and Conis, 2019; Sykes, 1958).

However, after all is said and done, education cannot be considered and viewed as a panacea for solving all the problems that exist in inmates or society; yet, it can set in motion the process of developing inmates' social psychology and a prosocial outlook on life, which is capable of helping them to address some of their problems to the benefits of not only themselves and immediate families and communities but also the larger society as a whole (e.g., Evans, 2018; Vandala, 2019; Ubah and Ubah, 2019; Linden, 2015; Bui and Morash, 2010; Ubah and Robinson, 2002: Jablecki, 2000; Austin, 1987). These insights suggest that improving an individual through education, no matter who that person is, will ultimately help society in the end.

In conclusion, as social-psychological development perspective suggests, it was the potential of correctional education programs in the rehabilitation process of prison inmates that made inmates' participation in correctional education program especially at the college levels the right step in the right direction in the transformation process of offender rehabilitation and reintegration efforts.

Opportunity Perspective

Opportunity perspective is another perspective that can be used in the attempts to justify college level correctional education programs (e.g., Vandala, 2019; Ubah and Ubah, 2019; Latessa et al., 2015; Cloward and Ohlin, 1960). This perspective suggests that most crimes, especially crimes on the street—which are usually carried out by poor, undereducated, and disenfranchised members of a society—can be explained by a lack of viable, legitimate means to the attainment of economic gains (i.e., external conditions) (Brown and Philo, 2017; Reiman and Leighton, 2017; Mutchnick and Lewis, 2017; Bui and Morash, 2010; Hipp et al., 2010; Herrschaft et al., 2009; Gaes, 2008; Ward and Maruna, 2007; Warner, 1999; Lockwood, 1991). Perhaps this notion originated with Merton's (1938) strain theory. Thus, strain theory postulates that deprivation, either absolute or relative, heightens feelings of anger, frustration, and confusion which in turn could result in crime (e.g., Barkan, 2018; Wang et al., 2010; Agnew, 2001; Bernard, 1990).

The opportunity perspective, therefore, suggests that acquiring college education credentials in prison will provide inmates with legitimate human capital (resources that influence future activities in people, such as marketable legitimate skills, trades, network relationships) that can open up better job opportunities, which in turn can build social bonds that protect against criminal behavior (e.g., Vandala, 2019; Ubah and Ubah, 2019; Brown and Philo, 2017; Mutchnick and Lewis, 2017; Bushway and Apel, 2012; Hipp et al., 2010; Wang et al., 2010; Herrschaft et al., 2009; Gaes, 2008; Kubrin and Stewart, 2006).

It has been documented that going to college enables one to obtain credentials for the labor market that could open considerable opportunities and social network relationships for social mobility (e.g., Barkan, 2018; Mutchnick and Lewis, 2017; Bui and Morash, 2010; Wang et al., 2010; Ubah and Robinson, 2002; Ellis and Lane, 1963). For example, Johnson (1964:610) postulates that "the higher the attainment of education, the greater one's earning power and the greater the possibility of improving one's station in life." Higher education credentials are known to help open up legitimate opportunity structures and wider positive social network relationships that can lead to decent living and considerable legitimate success and therefore could help reduce the pushes and pulls into street-level negative social resources and criminal capital (i.e., relationships with street-level nonconventional, antisocial people) (Weisburd et al., 2017; Mallender and Tierney, 2016; Dominguez and Raphael, 2015; Bui and Morash, 2010; Hipp et al., 2010; Wang et al., 2010; Kubrin and Stewart, 2006).

Based on this well-established finding, opportunity perspective suggests that inmates' completion of, or participation in, a college-level correctional education program is likely evidence of being engaged in the process of upward mobility, in the sense that such endeavor has the capacity to provide inmates with some necessary legitimate human and social capital resources (i.e., skills, knowledge, and network relationships) that can serve as a transformative and liberating force in their process of "going straight" and transforming from antisocial to pro-social behavior and hence positively impact their successful reintegration when released into the general society (Denney and Tynes, 2021; Vandala, 2019; Ubah and Ubah, 2019; Barkan, 2018; Evans, 2018; Mutchnick and Lewis, 2017; Kurlychek et al., 2012; Travis, 2005; Ubah and Robinson, 2002; Irwin, 1970).

Thus, Hershberger (1987) notes that education in prison is a vital link, a bridge for motivated inmates who are determined to move successfully from incarceration to the real world. With their new-found academic or vocational achievements, inmates would have the rudiments of new job skills that they can polish with further education or on-the-job training. With their success in an academic or vocational classroom, they develop social skills that are necessary for the workplace. Like education in the larger society, this idea of education in prison has some currency in the public arena not only at the national level but also at the global level as mandated in the United Nations Declarations, Standards and Conventions, as human rights for all people (Universal Declaration of Human Rights, 1948; UN Standard Minimum Rules for Treatment of Offenders, 1955); thus, former President Clinton states, "Education is the fault line, the great Continental Divide between those who will prosper and those who will not in the new economy" (Nicholas, 1996:14). Hershberger also states that inmates' educational successes in prison seem to have generalizing effects because they tend to serve as catalysts or "hooks" that compel ex-offenders to further their education and hence improve themselves outside of prison. Through correctional education, inmates would find the motivation to go on in their educational experience, and they may be able to improve their chances of staying out of prison after completing some courses (also see, for example, Vandala, 2019).

Perhaps, this assumption about the power of prison-based education in the liberating and transformative efforts of inmates is shared so greatly by no other group than the "Convict Criminology" movement. To be clear, "Convict Criminology primarily takes the shape of essays and empirical research by convicts or ex-convicts, in possession of a Ph.D. or on their way to completing one, or enlightened academics who make critiques of existing literature, policies, and practices, and contribute a new perspective on criminology, criminal justice, corrections, and community corrections" (Richards and Ross, 2001:180).

In part or in whole, the above assumptions of opportunity perspective on offender rehabilitation are in line with a major feature of the Good Live Model (GLM) of offender rehabilitation, which was developed in 2003 by Ward and Stewart, especially in the way the model analyzes the notion of criminogenic needs in terms of internal and external conditions (Latessa et al., 2015). Ward and Maruna (2007:160) stressed this idea very well by submitting that:

> In order to achieve primary goods effectively in particular circumstances, it is necessary to meet two sets of conditions. First, individuals require the capabilities or skills required to perform good-directed actions and, by doing so, engage in the valued activity or else reach it via a series of secondary steps. Second, in

> order to meet human needs, it is necessary to have access to relevant opportunities, and to be supported—or, at the very least, not thwarted—by others in the process. Deficits in either of these two sets of factors would therefore make it unlikely that a person would be able to achieve what he or her sets out to. He or she would be unable to have his or her needs met and therefore to secure the relevant primary goods. Criminogenic needs constitute the relevant deficits in the internal and external conditions.

Thus, there is a point in Ward and Maruna's assertion, and it has to do with the extent of the complexities in the offender desistance process and some of the complexities are discussed below in some details in form of weaknesses and challenges. Nevertheless, the individual change perspectives suggest that the provision of prison-based college education programs in correctional institutions indicates the right step in the right direction because the programs can promote change in some inmates, improve their psychological well-being, offer them credentials for the labor market, have potential for reducing recidivism rates and cost of incarceration, as well as improve economic status, public safety, and transformation of offenders into law-abiding citizens upon release. The premises of individual change perspectives form the arsenal, from which proponents of correctional education programs draw their arguments for the continued provision, funding, and improvement of prison-based college education programs (e.g., Denney and Tynes, 2021; Muhlhausen and Hurwitz, 2019; Ubah and Ubah, 2019). Regardless of the merits of the above strengths of individual change perspectives of offender rehabilitation and recidivism illuminated here, further consideration of the strengths of the perspectives is probably in order, to which we now turn.

STRENGTHS OF INDIVIDUAL CHANGE PERSPECTIVES OF OFFENDER REHABILITATION: A FURTHER LOOK

There has been inadequate analysis of the strengths of individual change perspectives of offender rehabilitation. The very few studies that have attempted to carry out such analysis, have done so in passing without much serious attention given to the strengths of the perspectives in ways that are critical enough. They seemed to stop precisely at a point where much more analysis of the strengths of the perspectives is needed. To fill the gap, a critical narrative of the strengths of the perspectives with a recognition of their weaknesses is carried out here. This analysis may be too important and too costly to ignore in 21st century corrections research, practice, and policy.

However, irrespective of the strengths of individual change perspectives of offender rehabilitation presented and analyzed in this book thus far, some questions remain and some of those questions include: (1) what are the additional strengths of individual change perspectives that can be considered; and (2) the importance of such considerations for criminology, criminal justice, and public policy in general and corrections in particular? The additional strengths of the perspectives that can be considered include, but may not be limited to, the recognition and appreciation of the idea that individual change perspectives of offender rehabilitation are part and parcel of the philosophies of crime causation and control that are commonly referred to in criminological literature as the "positivistic" tradition (i.e., one of the dominant traditions in criminology and sociology). In short, positivistic tradition are philosophies of crime causation and control that suggests that human behavior is shaped by individual and structural factors that can be identified through scientific methods rooted in the act of grouping and/or categorizing the subjects of interest (e.g., Ubah and Ubah, 2019; Barkan, 2018; Blevins, 2017; Lilly et al., 2010; Williams and McShane, 2010).

In the context of offender rehabilitation and reintegration processes, individual change perspectives form of positivistic tradition operate mainly under the assumption of the risk-need-responsivity (RNR) model (e.g., Latessa et al., 2015; Andrews et al., 2006). Risk-need-responsivity model of offender rehabilitation suggests that offenders' deficits and risks can be identified, manipulated, and managed with prison-based rehabilitation programs. That is, the programs have the propensity to enable offenders to acquire new, pro-social ways of feeling, thinking, and acting that could help mitigate the complexities of prison life and enable them in their process of trying to make a successful transition from prison into the larger society, as well as give them skills and trades that could enable them to aim their human goals and needs in legitimate, socially approved ways (Vandala, 2019; Ubah and Ubah, 2019; Evans, 2018; Latessa et al., 2015; Ward and Maruna, 2007).

By implication, the perspectives directly or indirectly suggest that education rehabilitation programs can help offenders manage their criminogenic needs and strive to meet their primary human needs in a socially acceptable way. As such, the perspectives are instruments for promoting primary human goods and needs (i.e., providing the offender with the essential ingredients for a good life) as well as reducing or avoiding risk for reoffending (e.g., Delisi and Conis, 2019; Vandala, 2019; Evans, 2018; Ward and Maruna, 2007). To be clear, moral development and social psychological development perspectives have more to do with internal conditions (i.e., skills, beliefs, attitudes, moral values, etc.), whereas the opportunity perspective is more in line with external conditions (i.e., opportunities, network relationships, supports, etc.) (Ubah and Ubah, 2019).

The perspectives collectively are optimistic about humanity with the view that the skills and trades offenders would gain from participating in rehabilitation programs could enable them to begin to see themselves differently than before and work toward transformation and transition from a criminal identity to a law-abiding one (e.g., Vandala, 2019; Evans, 2018; Latessa et al., 2015; Herrschaft et al., 2009). Ward and Maruna (2007:22) seem to capture this transformative and liberating process inmates can embark upon by postulating that "an important component of living an offense-free life appears to be viewing oneself as a different person with the capabilities and opportunities to achieve personally endorsed goals." This process has also been described as the "whole person" perspective (e.g., Ward and Stewart, 2003). The experience seems to be a necessary element in any transformative and enduring change process including, but not limited to, those embarked upon by offenders.

The technocratic language of the strengths of individual change perspectives of offender rehabilitation notwithstanding, a body of research has shown that the individual change perspectives of offender rehabilitation are not without certain underlying critical issues and questions of their own that challenged the degree of their usefulness or lack of it or both (e.g., Latessa et al., 2015; Herrschaft et al., 2009; McAdams, 1994; Veysey, 2008; Ward and Maruna, 2007; Ubah, 2003). The questions, then, are: (1) what are these issues in individual change perspectives of offender rehabilitation; and (2) what is the importance of such issues for criminology, criminal justice, and public policy?

Critical Issues in Individual Change Perspectives

Critical issues in individual change perspectives include, but are not limited to, the charge that the perspectives operate under flawed assumptions, such as: that offenders are essentially different from all other human groups; that reducing offender problems will reduce criminal behavior; that if services are made available, offenders will use them; that services actually accomplish what they are designed to do; that the perspectives fail to specify the length of inmate exposure, which can lead to a reduction in recidivism; that, in terms of perceived differences between men and women, the perspectives fail to specify which process tends to work better for men and for women when applying them; that the perspectives are stated so cautiously as to raise the question of whether any available data could show any one of them to be preferable to others; and that generally one may wonder how education, which so often seems ineffective in the general society, has the capacity to accomplish so much under the harsh conditions of prison life (e.g., Ubah, 2003).

Furthermore, there is the issue that individual change perspectives are limited in their utility because they are narrow and not broad in nature. As a result, they have been described as "local theories of change" and not "complete rehabilitation theories" (Ward and Maruna, 2007). Thus, Ward and Maruna (2007:33) offered a summation of what they believe constitutes a complete rehabilitation theory:

> A complete "rehabilitation theory" is broader in nature and refers to the overarching aims, values, principles, justifications, and etiological assumptions that are used to guide interventions and help therapists translate these rather abstract principles into practice. Rehabilitation theory, therefore, is essentially a hybrid theory comprised of values, core principles, etiological assumptions, and practice guidelines. In effect, it contains elements of normative, etiological and practice/treatment theories within it while being somewhat broader than the sum of these parts. It contains multiple levels and enables correctional workers to intervene in diverse but coherent ways.

Lessons from the Issues of Individual Change Perspectives

The lessons learned from the critical issues and questions surrounding individual change perspectives of offender rehabilitation, and the importance of such lessons for criminology, criminal justice, and public policy and practice, are insightful and instructive in that it is conceivable that, with regard to the reduction of recidivism, the program's principles and assumptions matter because some types, levels, and process of prison-based educational programs, for example, may be more effective than others (e.g., Anderson, 1981; Brennan, 2012; Cronbach, 1982; Cullen, 2005; Herrschaft et al., 2009; Marlowe, 2006; Martinson, 1974, 1976; Veysey, 2008). This is so because "education should not be viewed as some uniform and homogenous entity exposure to which gives skills and alters thinking and motivation invariably in the same fashion" (Ubah, 2002:18).

Emphasizing the limits of individual change perspectives, McAdams (1994) attests that a person's personality involves three domains: traits, personal strivings, and self-narratives. Ward and Maruna (2007) reveal that prison-based rehabilitation programs that are informed and grounded by individual change perspectives operate mainly from the assumption of the risk-need-responsivity (RNR) model, which overly views offenders from the risk lens and his or her criminogenic needs while giving discretionary and not mandatory attention to the individual's whole personality attributes (i.e., the humanity of offenders). In attesting to the weakness of programs informed by these perspectives, Herrschaft et al (2009:467) postulate that "these types of programs often disregard the ability of an offender to personally initiate positive change during the reentry process. Reentry programs commonly treat desistance as a conclusive event. They operate under the assumption that offender needs to be fixed by an external agent because they are incapable of doing so themselves."

By overemphasizing on the offender's criminogenic personality traits, RNR model perspectives neglect the important role of the other two levels of personality in the individual's life course. Ward and Maruna (2007:84) seem to epitomize this situation by postulating that "the other two domains of personality (both neglected in RNR model) tend to be the more dynamic and agentic (that is, at the control of the individual actor). As such, these two levels of personality present the best opportunity for changing personality over the life course." These observations seem to form the premise of a growing body of literature challenging the assumptions of RNR model (e.g., Latessa et al., 2015; Herrschaft et al., 2009; McAdams, 1994; Veysey, 2008; Ward and Maruna, 2007). The suggestions of this emerging literature on RNR model can be captured in the following assertion by Ward and Maruna (2007:105):

> The narrowness of its basic assumptions and value commitments means that the primary etiological elements of RNR revolve around the detection and role of risk factors in the generation of crime. The failure of RNR explicitly to consider a broader range of human needs and the role of identity and agency in offending means that it ultimately pays insufficient attention to core therapeutic and intervention tasks (e.g., treatment alliance, motivational issues).

By focusing too much on the criminogenic personality needs of offenders, the individual change perspectives fail to sufficiently consider that humans are active, goal-seeking beings with the capacity to detect and pursue human needs and goods (e.g., Latessa et al., 2015; Brennan, 2012; Ward and Maruna, 2007). This strength-based idea of the Good Lives Model (GLM) is in line with the perspective of niche construction which emulates from gene-culture co-evolution theory developed by Odling-Smee and colleagues (2003). Niche construction suggests that organisms, in their striving for primary human needs and goods, have the capacity to alter their environment and thereby modify the relationship between their characteristics and the features of their environment. These insights and lessons on the capacity and agency of human beings are very important and, as such, need to be seriously taken into account in any individual change perspectives considerations. Unfortunately, it has not been the case thus far with individual change perspectives of offender rehabilitation.

It seems another issue with individual change perspectives was that they lack external consistency about human functioning. This is so because the perspectives fail to sufficiently consider the contextual nature of human behavior. As a result, they present general principles that are applied without adequate consideration of the social contexts and macro-economic forces impacting returning offenders lives (e.g., Denney and Tynes, 2021; Kirk, 2012; Bui and Morash, 2010; Hipp et al., 2010; Kubrin and Stewart, 2006; Maruna, 2012; Ward and Maruna, 2007; Miller, 2012). The need for adequate consideration of all these interacting social processes in the successful offender desistance efforts matters greatly, but unfortunately it seems to be seriously underplayed in the individual change perspectives assumptions. But if any individual change perspectives had the capacity and great promise to pay sufficient attention to this issue, perhaps opportunity perspective probably is (e.g., Clark et al., 2020; Ubah, 2003).

For instance, in their study entitled "Parolee Recidivism in California: The Effect of Neighborhood Context and Social Service Agency Characteristics," Hipp et al., (2010) not only underline the importance of adequately considering the social context in which offenders return but also the socioeconomic context and the context of nearby neighborhoods. They accounted for not only the economic characteristics of the census tract to which offenders return but also other structural characteristics of those tracts. Ward and Maruna (2007:82) underscore the importance of this consideration and their interacting processes by asserting that "because human beings are interdependent and rely on other people and social institutions to function, care should be taken to ensure any treatment plan takes into account the contexts in which offenders are likely to be released." Recognizing the interacting social processes of those contexts of returning offenders and adequately accounting for them are important in a desistence effort because human beings are interdependent and rely on other people and social institutions in their context to function. As such, it is imperative that care is taken to ensure that any rehabilitation idea takes into accounts the contexts in which offenders are likely to be returned (e.g., Delisi and Conis, 2019; Krisberg et al., 2019; Morenoff and Harding, 2014; Hipp et al., 2010; Travis, 2005). Unfortunately, that critical lesson seems not to be given sufficient consideration by individual change perspectives of offender rehabilitation.

SUMMARY

This chapter argues that individual change perspectives, such as moral development perspective, social psychological development perspective, and opportunity perspective, are part and parcel of the philosophies of crime causation and control that are most referred to in the criminological literature as the "positivistic" tradition (Lilly et al., 2010; Williams and McShane, 2014).

Such perspectives operate mainly under the assumption of the risk-need-responsivity (RNR) model of offender rehabilitation (e.g., see Latessa et al., 2015; Andrews et al., 2006), which suggests that offenders' deficits and risks can be identified, manipulated, and managed with prison-based rehabilitation programs: that the programs have the propensity to enable offenders to acquire new, pro-social ways of feeling, thinking, and acting; and that the programs can give offenders skills and trades necessary to enable them to earn their human goals and needs in a legitimate socially approved ways (Ward and Maruna, 2007).

In other words, these individual change perspectives are instrumental means of promoting primary human goods and needs (i.e., providing the offender with the essential ingredients for a good life) as well as reducing or avoiding risk for reoffending. By implication, the perspectives directly or indirectly suggest that education rehabilitation programs can help offenders manage their criminogenic needs and strive to meet their primary human needs in a socially acceptable way. It is noteworthy to point out that moral development and social psychological development perspectives have more to do with internal conditions (i.e., skills, beliefs, attitudes, moral values, etc.), whereas the opportunity perspective is more in line with external conditions (i.e., opportunities, network relationships, supports, etc.).

Collectively, the perspectives seem to suggest that the skills and trades offenders would gain from participating in rehabilitation programs could enable them to begin to see themselves differently than before and work toward transformation and transition from a criminal identity to a law-abiding one (Herrschaft et al., 2009). Thus, Ward and Maruna (2007:22) posit that "an important component of living an offense-free life appears to be viewing oneself as a different person with the capabilities and opportunities to achieve personally endorsed goals." This approach has also been described as the "whole person" perspective (e.g., Ward and Stewart, 2003). The experience seems to be a necessary element in any enduring change process including, but not limited to, those embarked upon by offenders.

To some extent, individual change perspectives seem to have merit in the tradition of post-modernism, social constructionism, and critical realism. Ward and Maruna (2007) probably captured that connection very well by asserting that the elements of these philosophies of science (i.e., post-modernism, social constructionism, and critical realism) seem to form the foundation of individual change perspectives and, in effect, are part and parcel of the hybrid of these philosophies of science, thus comprising some of their values, principles, etiological assumptions, and perhaps practical guidelines.

The perspectives seem to offer interesting ideas about offender rehabilitation and recidivism process, yet, notwithstanding the strengths of individual change perspectives of offender rehabilitation, when the perspectives are examined critically, some serious issues and questions that point to the negative aspects are raised. Recognizing and understanding such weaknesses of individual change perspectives of offender rehabilitation are important because, for one thing, such endeavors would enable us to have broader and deeper insights and lessons on the perspectives and perhaps encourage a much more serious attention and imagination to be given to the issues for the benefit of research, policy, and practice.

Such endeavor of recognizing and understanding the weaknesses of individual change perspectives of offender rehabilitation was explored in this chapter in detail. For instance, it has been shown here that the issues include, but are not limited to, the charge that the perspectives operate under flawed assumptions, such as that offenders are essentially different from all other human groups; that reducing offender problems will reduce criminal behavior; that if services are made available, offenders will use them; that services actually accomplish what they are designed to do; that the perspectives fail to specify the length of inmate exposure, which can lead to a reduction in recidivism; that in terms of perceived differences between men and women the perspectives fail to specify which process tends to work better for men and for women when applying them; that the perspectives are stated so cautiously as to raise the question of whether any available data could show any one of them to be preferable to others; and that generally one may wonder how education, which so often seems ineffective in the general society, has the capacity to accomplish so much under the harsh conditions of prison life (Ubah and Ubah, 2019).

Furthermore, that individual change perspectives are limited in their utility because they are narrow and not broad in nature. As a result, they have been described as "local theories of change" and not "complete rehabilitation theories" (Ward and Maruna, 2007). That focusing too much on the criminogenic personality needs of offenders, the individual change perspectives fail to sufficiently consider that humans are active, goal-seeking beings with the capacity to detect and pursue human needs and goods (e.g., Latessa et al., 2015; Brennan, 2012; Ward and Maruna, 2007).

An insightful and instructive set of lessons has been learned from the issues and questions surrounding individual change perspectives of offender rehabilitation and the importance of such lessons for criminology, criminal justice, public policy, and practice. Nonetheless, the need to critically continue to think and rethink the issues of this subject is paramount for criminology, criminal justice, public policy and practice, and, as such, more studies need to be conducted on the subjects. Such studies are essential for deeper knowledge of criminology, criminal justice, and public policy and practice as they might provide further critical insights and lessons into the issues concerning the strengths and weaknesses of individual change perspectives of offender rehabilitation and recidivism for a better service delivery of activities and practice as well as systematic research projects.

As important as the lessons learned and insights gleaned from the discussions of the issues of individual change perspectives of offender rehabilitation thus far, it might be imperative to take a closer look at the issues pessimistic worldview of offender rehabilitation reacted to, which the chapter that follows discusses in detail.

Chapter 3

Pessimistic Reaction to Individual Change

Perspectives of Offender Rehabilitation

A CLOSER LOOK AT THE ISSUES PESSIMISTIC WORLDVIEW REACTED TO

In contrast to the individual change perspectives of offender rehabilitation is the pessimistic worldview (Martinson, 1974). Pessimistic reaction to individual change perspectives is the antithesis of the rehabilitative ideal of offender rehabilitation. Martinson's 1974 article, "What Works? Questions and Answers About Prison Reform," is the most pessimistic reaction literature to individual change perspectives' reference point and one of the most cited criminological literatures on corrections. Scholars of the pessimistic persuasion argue that offender rehabilitation programs such as prison-based correctional education programs do not work as proponents of rehabilitative ideals want us to believe. Therefore, scholars who embrace this perspective recommend the elimination of correctional education programs in the U.S. penal systems.

The issues in the individual change perspectives that were reacted to by the pessimistic worldview were identified in detail in the previous chapter. They include, but may not be limited to, the charge that the perspectives operate under flawed assumptions such as that offenders are essentially different from all other human groups; that reducing offender problems will reduce criminal behavior; that if services are made available, offenders will use them; that services actually accomplish what they are designed to do; that the perspectives fail to specify the length of inmate exposure, which can lead to a reduction in recidivism; that in terms of perceived differences between men and women, the perspectives fail to specify which process tends to work better for men and for women when applying them.

Furthermore, it is charged that the perspectives are stated so cautiously as to raise the question of whether any available data could show any one of them to be preferable to others; and that generally one may wonder how education, which so often seems ineffective in the general society, has the capacity to accomplish so much under the harsh conditions of prison life (Ubah and Ubah, 2019). Also, it is charged that individual change perspectives are limited in their utility because they are narrow and not broad in nature. As a result, they have been described as "local theories of change" and not "complete rehabilitation theories" (Ward and Maruna, 2007). For more detailed identification of the issues and questions in individual change perspectives of offender rehabilitation please see chapter 2 of this book.

MAGNIFYING THE PESSIMISTIC REACTION: A CLOSER LOOK

As chapter 3 depicts, there is a growing body of literature challenging the strength-based approach of individual change perspectives on offender rehabilitation (e.g., Bui and Morash, 2010; Herrschaft et al., 2009; Martinson, 1974; Maruna and Ward, 2007; Maruna and LeBel, 2003; Maruna, 2001; Travis, 2005; Veysey, 2008; Ward and Maruna, 2007).

Perhaps the most definitive pessimistic reaction that challenges the individual-change perspectives of rehabilitative programs in prisons is the survey by Lipton, Martinson, and Wilks (1975) of the results of prison-reform programs for adult men offenders between 1945 and 1967. From this survey, Martinson (1974) spun off a controversial article in which he assessed several rehabilitative studies to answer the general question of "What works?" in prison reform. He analyzed several studies supporting the notion that rehabilitative programs do not work, as well as other studies that support the position that rehabilitative programs are effective. In addition, he criticized those studies that appear not to support the pessimistic view of the usefulness of rehabilitative programs. He did so by charging those studies with producing no clear pattern to indicate the efficacy of any methods of treatment and summarized his findings by concluding that "with few and isolated exceptions, the rehabilitative efforts that have been reported so far have had no appreciable effect on recidivism" (Martinson, 1974:25).

Martinson's article, which was titled "What Works? Questions and Answers About Prison Reform," became known as the "nothing works" report (e.g., Latessa et al., 2015; Paparozzi and Guy, 2014; Cullen and Gilbert, 2013; Delisi and Conis, 2013; Welch, 1996). The conclusion that nothing works had considerable impact on the academic and public discussion over inmate rehabilitative programs. Martinson's "nothing works" article became the pessimistic-camp reference point, indeed one of the most cited criminological literatures. Critics of the rehabilitative ideal embraced eagerly the "nothing works" verdict to help justify abandoning rehabilitation and redirecting American correctional philosophy and practice to the new epoch of deterrence and incapacitation (Delisi and Conis, 2013; Latessa et al., 2015; Gendreau, 1996). It is important to note that, contrary to popular opinion, Lipton, Martinson, and Wilks (1975) did not make the sweeping claim that nothing works. Rather, they cited positive outcomes in 48 percent of the programs evaluated. The important question, then, is how can one describe Martinson's sweeping conclusion as "nothing works" when some things really did work?

This author suggests that Martinson's (1974) "nothing works" conclusion regarding rehabilitative efforts on corrections was a carnival-mirror image conclusion concerning the results of rehabilitative efforts. A carnival mirror is a mirror that hides as much as it reveals (Reiman and Leighton, 2017; Reiman, 2004). It is a carnival-mirror conclusion in the sense that Martinson's conclusion did not show the complete picture of correctional rehabilitation efforts. By focusing mainly on the dark and giving little or no attention to the encouraging side of the entire picture, the "nothing works" conclusion distorted and continues to distort the image of the results of offender-rehabilitation efforts in that the "nothing works" rhetoric and conclusion are usually the major bases of argument and reference points for critics of offender rehabilitation.

Perhaps it is equally important to note that Martinson (1979) revisited some of his earlier conclusions on offender rehabilitation. At this time, he concluded somewhat differently from his earlier (1974) assessment. He reported that some rehabilitative programs were indeed beneficial and that some treatment programs did have an appreciable effect on recidivism. Yet Martinson's later (partial) change of mind received little attention compared with the splash made by his earlier evaluation. Thus, "It is ironic, but instructive, that whereas Martinson's 1974 nothing works article is among the most cited of criminological writings, his revisionist 1979 essay earned scant attention" (Welch, 1996:100). One is tempted to conclude that the later position failed whereas the earlier one succeeded, not because of the merits lacking in the reviewed argument but because of its failure to be in tune with a climate of opinion increasingly frustrated with and hostile to a rehabilitative approach.

As one would expect, Martinson's (1974) study is not without critics of its own. For example, Palmer (1975) argues that Martinson's study is characterized by bias, inconsistency, and omissions of facts regarding the somewhat optimistic assessment of intensive-supervision programs that have provided the most encouraging reports on offender rehabilitation. Palmer notes that throughout Martinson's correctional education assessment, he was mostly interested in assessing the total efficacy of each given, prison-based, education program as a sum total of a program's effects on all the variables that had been studied. Palmer concludes that this criterion of a universally effective program was "a search for the impossible."

Perhaps Cullen and Gendreau (1989:24) provided the more useful perspective for an understanding of the idiosyncrasies underlying the negative interpretations of Martinson's (1974) work by suggesting that "the rejection of rehabilitation has less to do with a careful reading of empirical literature and more to do with changes in the social fabric that triggered a corresponding shift in thinking about corrections." Perhaps there is no better indication of the change perceived by Cullen and Gendreau than the debate over prison-based Pell Grants for correctional education programs. This debate is examined in detail in chapter 9.

In addition to Martinson's (1974) insights, the issues raised in the literature can be magnified further with a closer look at the acknowledgment of the problems of "self-selection" in the study of subjects that participated in correctional education programs (e.g., Denney and Tynes, 2021; Bushway and Apel, 2012; Brennan, 2012; Piquero, 2012; Anderson, 1981).

The case of self-selection is very serious because it raises the question of whether the actual participation in the correctional education program (i.e., deficit based) or the motivation to participate in the program (i.e., strength based) is much more responsible for the impact on recidivism. One is attempted to argue that the motivation to participate in the program is much more responsible for the impact on recidivism than the actual participation in the program. This is because offender participation in correctional education programs does not result in greater readiness not to recidivate to the life of crime. Instead, the increased readiness not to recidivate and the interest in participating in correctional programs are the result of the offenders' decision to do what it takes to bring their lives into order—perhaps a way they are signaling their willingness to desist from future offending (e.g., see Vandala, 2019; Brennan, 2012; Bushway and Apel, 2012; Maruna, 2012; Piquero, 2012).

In her "Rethinking Reentry" article, Veysey (2008:3) makes an interesting observation that "the importance of what people bring to the change endeavor cannot be underestimated. The largest predictor set is the intangibles that people bring with them. The second most important is the human connection reflected in the therapeutic relationship." Veysey postulates that 15 percent can be attributed to the intervention itself, 30 percent to educators with excellent relational skills, 15 percent to hope, and 40 percent to individual strengths, resources, and desires. This observation and the insight Veysey provided suggest that the power of personal agency people bring to the change process is perhaps the most important in whether they will succeed in the process.

What may be at work in the dynamics of a change process may have more to do with some general restructuring of outlook, perhaps a sort of conversion, as such, that may be the main factor in determining whether a previously incarcerated and released offender will recidivate; whether that offender participated in a correctional treatment program or not appears to be more of an indicator of the presence of such a new outlook than its cause. After all, if an offender participated in a correctional rehabilitation program but had not really decided to "go straight" when released into the larger society, that offender would be most likely to go back to the life of crime. On the other hand, if an offender did not participate in correctional programming because of a lack of opportunity or participated in a program but had already decided to "go straight" anyway, it is more likely that when that offender is released into the general community he or she would not engage in antisocial behavior. Piquero (2012:45) raises some interesting issues that seem to underscore the point in question here by asserting that:

> What are we to do with offenders who are not in facilities that have these employment training programs? What about offenders who are in facilities that have inadequate employment training programs—much less any useful programming because of today's constrained correctional budgets? Offenders in both of these instances would not have had any opportunity to be an employment program graduate. Does that make them any less employable or any less a desister after release from prison?

From the standpoint of pessimistic perspectives, the answer to the question is no. Because after all, lack of participation in a correctional program can mean several things, such as the lack of opportunity to get into the program or the lack of willingness to go straight, or both. It is important to keep in mind that the lack of opportunity to participate in a correctional rehabilitative program or participation in a half-baked program does not go hand in hand with the lack of willingness not to go straight. It simply means that the offender could not participate in a meaningful correctional program due to lack of chance or opportunity to do so. After all, correctional authorities are gatekeepers of who participates in one program or another and who does not. Sometimes these programs may serve as incentives that prison authorities can use to control inmates toward greater conformity to the rules and regulations of the penitentiary. Thus, access control to participation in correctional programs provides prison authorities with a form of positive sanction which is crucial for maintaining order in prison (Colvin, 1992; Taylor and Tewksbury, 2002; Ubah and Ubah, 2013).

As Veysey (2008:3) instructs, offender rehabilitation programs in many ways are no different than medical, psychiatric, or substance abuse treatment, and literature on these fields reveals that:

> How illness is embedded in the life narrative has important implications for recovery. Persons who believe they will recover or who have narrative that find positive meaning in the illness experience are more likely to survive life-threatening illnesses than those who don't. While it is unclear what physiological mechanisms are at work to produce the puzzling result, this same phenomenon is repeatedly observed in other disciplines whether it is called a placebo effect, a Hawthorne effect, or is ascribed to unmeasured personal characteristics.

Veysey (2008:5) goes on to say that:

> Even if we were to be able to create the perfect set of comprehensive and integrated services targeted to what former prisoners want and need, "fixing" offenders' problems only bring them halfway back. Reentry programs may accomplish the role exit component, but do not address the role entry component. Telling someone to stop being criminal may work for a period, but that person needs a replacement identity, and this identity may be chosen only by the individual who is in the process of change. Only offenders can accomplish the changes necessary to become a productive member of society. No matter how coercive or punitive, corrections can't do it nor can treatment. The most these organizations can do is to create the environments and conditions in which change is likely to occur.

In such a case, contrary to the individual change perspectives assumption, offender participation or lack of participation in a correctional rehabilitation program is not, and cannot be, the main determining factor of whether that offender will recidivate to the life of crime or not. Instead, having embraced a new attitude toward life is the main determining factor. This is so because even if an offender had the opportunity to participate in a correctional program but did not want to change from his or her criminal ways of life, participation by itself would not make any difference on how that offender would perform in the future. After all, some inmates participate in correctional education programs just for the sake of trying to gain parole and not genuinely willing not to recidivate to their criminogenic culture (false positive) when released from the society of captives into the general society (Latessa et al., 2015; Piquero, 2012; Ubah, 2002; Wilson, 2005). Assuming that individual change perspectives assumption has promise in the offender rehabilitation process, generally one may wonder how education, which so often seems ineffective in the general society, has the capacity to accomplish so much under the harsh conditions of prison life (Ubah, 2003).

After all this is said and done, this is not to suggest that "nothing works" with correctional education programs. Rather, the issues raised here point to the realities of the challenges and complexities of human nature in general and correctional treatment programs in particular, and as such, they remind us of the need to continue thinking critically and deeply about ways to improve our efforts and delivery of offender rehabilitation programs in our penal systems. Overall, the problematic issues of individual change perspectives pointed out here suggest that their explicit focus on risks and needs of offenders may be a necessary but not a sufficient condition for achieving an enduring desistance from future criminal behavior. Nonetheless, assuming that the idealistic perspectives have relevance for offender treatment, is there empirical evidence supporting the usefulness of these perspectives? On that note, we turn to such examination after the following summary.

SUMMARY

In sum, the pessimistic perspectives argue that the rehabilitative theories are stated so cautiously as to raise the question whether any available data could show any one of them to be preferable to others. Simply put, the idealistic theories are speculative and not specific enough regarding the relationship between prison-based education programming and offender recidivism.

It is clear that cumulative pessimistic efforts that eventually led to the elimination of prison-based education Pell Grants in 1994 with the passage of the Crime Bill were much encouraged by the negative interpretations of Martinson's (1974) article by critics of correctional education programming.

It seems that the pessimistic reaction of conservative politicians regarding prison-based offender rehabilitation did succeed in their political agenda mainly because of the changes in the social fabric that triggered a corresponding shift in thinking about corrections—a thinking that is in tune with a climate of opinion increasingly frustrated with and hostile to a rehabilitative approach.

Finally, when all is said and done, it is clear that the debate over prison-based education has not been resolved. Instead, it continues to divide scholars, policy makers, correctional practitioners, and the public in general. A case in point is the debate generated by the Second Chance Act and Second Chance Pell Pilot Initiative that partially started to fund some college in prison programs once again.

Chapter 4

A Critical Examination of Empirical Evidence of Offender Rehabilitation-Correctional Education

THE EXAMINATION PARADIGM

It is a truism that there is a large body of research literature on the general subject of offender rehabilitation. However, not all this empirical literature is directly relevant for this examination. The literature reviewed here was selected because of two major principles: One, the studies must specifically deal with prison-based the postsecondary educational rehabilitation program; and, two, the studies must meet certain criteria suggested by Gerber and Fritsch (1995) as highly appropriate in this kind of research. These criteria include:

1. The study must report empirical data.
2. The study must make use of sampling of subjects such as matching the subjects on certain variables/characteristics, random selection of subjects where possible, or making use of treatment and control groups. Here a control group is defined as a comparison group composed of ex-inmates who did not participate in the college educational programs (nonparticipants) or participated but did not complete any of the programs attempted (noncompleters).
3. The use of tests of statistical significance to determine the status of observed differences in the dependent variable between groups, instead of assuming that such differences are due to chance.

The above three deciding factors for the selection of literature for review were employed to keep the focus of this book narrowly limited to the correctional-educational aspect of offender rehabilitation, and to make sure that the empirical studies selected for review go beyond impressionistic and methodically uncontrolled observation. Based on these factors, a considerable number of studies that did not meet the criteria were excluded from this examination.

The principles utilized for the selection of relevant literature differ from what most studies on the subject use (for example, see Scott, 2018; Kim and Clark, 2013; Burke and Vivian, 2001; Robinson, 1990; Martinson, 1974). The bulk of these studies are more concerned with different aspects of offender rehabilitation than this examination. Many of those studies utilize methodically flawed techniques (White et al, 2022; Scott, 2018; Kim and Clark, 2013), and some have a very broad focus, as was the case with Martinson's (1974) controversial review which assessed the literature on offender rehabilitation published between 1945 through 1967. Martinson examined both prison-based rehabilitative literature and community-based programs. He analyzed correctional education studies, offender counseling studies, medical treatment studies, deincarceration studies, et al. The excessive broadness of the approach used by Martinson is one of the aspects of his report that has been criticized heavily by several scholars (e.g., Palmer, 1975; Reiman, 1995; Welch, 1996; Ubah, 2002). Yet it seems that Martinson's broad focus may have been appropriate. For the less ambitious purpose of this book, however, the focus will be appropriately narrowed.

The studies reviewed here will for the most part be discussed one after another instead of collectively. The rationale behind this approach was to enable a thorough review of the studies by explicating their methods, their results, their strengths and weaknesses, their substance, and lessons to be learned individually and the importance of those lessons for criminology, criminal justice, and public policy.

The empirical studies examined below are broken down into three groups: those published before, during, and after Martinson's investigative period; they are arranged according to year of publication from earlier ones to recent ones. This ordering or pattern will reveal such trends as there may be concerning findings, substantive nature, and the nature of the methodologies of the selected studies.

PRE-MARTINSON'S 1974 STUDIES OF PRISON-BASED EDUCATION PROGRAMS IMPACT ASSESSMENT

Martinson chose 1945 as the starting year for his famous comprehensive review of studies conducted on offender rehabilitation; it would be interesting to know the state of correctional education literature before Martinson's "nothing works" conclusion. Because of the narrow focus of the present investigation, however, efforts to identify relevant pre-Martinson literature on prison-based education programs proved abortive. Martinson noted in his 1974 report on offender rehabilitation that his study was the first comprehensive account of what was known about offender rehabilitation. He then seems to imply that no empirical literature on the issues exists before 1945. To set the record straight, the truth of the matter is that there are several empirical studies on offender rehabilitation published before 1945. These studies (about 11 of them) were identified and reviewed by Bailey (1966) in his work "Correctional Outcome: An Evaluation of 100 Reports."

However, none of the 11 pre-1945 studies reviewed by Bailey was included in this study, since they fall outside its focus. Bailey's (1966) review was on the general subject of offender rehabilitation, just like Martinson's review.

A REVIEW OF IMPACT ASSESSMENT STUDIES PUBLISHED WITHIN MARTINSON'S 1974 INVESTIGATIVE PERIODS 1945–1967

Martinson's (1974) study reveals that there is not much more than a handful of empirical analyses evaluating prison-based education programs published within the study period, 1945 through 1967. From these studies, this author selected the five that are reviewed below.

The first study of interest was conducted by A. C. Schnur (1948), who carried out an investigation of a minimum security institution's academic/vocational educational programming to determine the effect of prisoners' exposure to education on recidivism by measuring post-release parole status in relation to prison school attendance and nonattendance. A criterion group of 1,762 men, subdivided into those who attended prison school for less than six (but more than two) months and those who attended for more than six (and up to 12 months), was compared to a control group of 1,082 men who did not. The measurement period for recidivism was two years.

Findings indicate no significant difference in recidivism rates between the control group and the criterion group with less than six months schooling. However, Schnur found that significant difference existed in recidivism rates between the control group and the experimental group members with over six months of school attendance.

The main lesson learned from this evaluation is its suggestion of a minimum length of schooling that may be enough to make a difference for inmate participants. The large sample size of the study inspires some confidence in this finding. However, the lack of information on the nature of the educational programs studied may be seen as a limitation. Perhaps a more serious limitation of this study is its failure to call attention to the problem of self-selection of the program participants, i.e., the possibility that participants are mainly inmates already otherwise predisposed to rehabilitate themselves.

Next to Schnur's study was Fox's (1950). Fox set out to determine the efficacy of a vocational school program in a minimum security prison in terms of failure and success of men on parole and in terms of monetary cost of the program. An experimental group consisting of 144 men who were in the minimum security facility for a two-year period and attended vocational school was compared to a control group of 144 men with no school attendance in a maximum security facility.

The control group was formed in a way that represents men who would have been eligible for placement on the school program if they had been in the minimum security facility. The measurement period was based on the monthly reports of the progress and violation of men while on parole. Fox's findings were consistent and statistically highly significant in favor of men from the minimum security institution, both from the standpoint of successes and failures of parole.

The strength of this study could be claimed to rest on the way the control group was chosen—by individually matching selected attributes of men in the control group with similar attributes of men in the criterion group so that the dividing characteristics of the two groups were reduced to a great extent; yet it is a serious limitation of this study that the two groups came from different security-level institutions. Presumably the two institutions are different with respect to the type of offenders each facility holds, and it cannot be taken for granted that the effect of education is the same for different types of offenders.

Minimum security institutions hold low-level offenders, while maximum prisons hold hard-core offenders and those hard to discipline. If inmates can be rehabilitated, those in minimum security institutions are often viewed as better candidates for rehabilitation than inmates in maximum security facilities (Clemmer, 1958; Sykes, 1958). It is then not at all clear what sort of conclusions can be validly drawn from this study. The sample utilized was small; it also fails to provide any information on the nature of the educational programs offered and therefore allows no inference as to the precise cause(s) of the observed results.

Zink (1962) examined post-release parolee tendencies in relation to their participation or nonparticipation in prison academic programs at the New Castle Minimum Correctional Institution in Wilmington, Delaware. A criterion group of 110 inmates who attended school for at least two months while in prison was compared to a control group of 110 inmates of nonattenders. Three to five years post-release was used as the examination period. The post-release criminal tendencies studied include arrests, convictions, and sentences.

Results indicate that in the three-, four-, and five-year time periods studied, consistent differences in post-release criminality existed, favoring the school group members. The differences were statistically significant at the .05 level of confidence, all in favor of the school participants.

The strength of this study is the selection of control and experimental groups matched to make them similar in terms of individual and group characteristics. In addition, Zink (1962) notes that the Federal Bureau of Investigation (FBI) measuring instrument, which he regarded as the most accurate instrument for follow-up reports, was used to determine post-release conduct of the members of the two groups. However, the FBI uses several instruments in measuring crime and criminality, and Zink failed to describe what instrument he was referring to and what it entails (White et al., 2022; United States Sentencing Commission, 2016; Steurer et al., 2001).

Furthermore, another possible limitation of this study has to do with its failure to differentiate the inmate groups classified as program participants. Program participants encompass inmates who completed the programs and those who did not (perhaps this is insignificant since a mere two months' participation was enough to qualify a program participant). Furthermore, important issues like the length of the academic programs studied and how inmates got into the programs were not addressed. Thus, a qualitative knowledge of the programs studied could have helped in this regard. Like Fox's study, discussed above, the sample size of this study is also small, which raises the question of whether these findings can be generalized to the general inmate population.

In another follow-up study of parolees from Marion Minimum Correctional Security Institution in Ohio, Cochran (1965) reported that there was a difference in the success rates of parolees who participated in the academic or vocational school program versus nonparticipants. This difference was significant at the .01 level.

The population for this study was 234. The criterion group consisted of 117 men who had been involved in the education program and was compared with 117 men with no school attendance. Although the control group for this study was randomly selected, the experimental group was not. Rather, the researcher, using unspecified criteria, personally chose a limited number of the parolees that made up the experimental group instead of using all who qualified for it or a random selection from the total. A technique of this nature in composing a sample in this kind of research has the tendency to produce bias that is likely to affect the findings of the study. This is probably the most serious shortcoming in the study of these subjects. Another limitation of the study could also relate to the fact that the survey measured recidivism within only one year after release from prison, probably not enough time to determine the effect of the exposure to education.

In addition, the study also lacked a differential educational classification (program participants of parolees) and did not talk about the length of programs studied. These were the same problems that were pointed out with Zink's study.

LESSONS LEARNED FROM THE EMPIRICAL STUDIES OF 1945–1967

Taken as a whole, the studies reviewed from 1945 through 1967 in some way seem to support the idealistic position rather than the pessimistic one concerning the rehabilitative power of higher education programs in prison. While they do suffer from various defects, they nevertheless seem to show that acquiring correctional education can make a significant difference in the recidivism rates of parolees.

Do the results of the above studies provide sufficient ground for arguing that Martinson was wrong in his conclusion that nothing works? Probably not, because the studies reviewed above were just a handful when compared to the total of 231 offender rehabilitation studies examined by Martinson. However, one can conclude that the above studies lend support to the idea that participation in such programs (i.e., prison-based education) apparently serves to differentiate the more successful parolees from the unsuccessful ones. This conclusion, however, leaves open the question of whether exposure to secondary-level education in prison has a causal impact on parolees' tendency to recidivate.

Another lesson learned from the above review is the identification of common flaws to which investigators need to be aware when conducting future studies on the subject. These flaws include the utilization of an undifferentiated criterion groups (program completers versus noncompleters), which makes it impossible for anyone to determine whether the two groups involved have different recidivism rates, and the use of a weak control group. It is desirable that studies of this kind clearly define or separate the criterion groups referred to as program participants. This is because program participants include program completers and noncompleters. These two parolee groups are different from one another in terms of their level of education and, for the sake of clarity, should not be classified as one group.

There was also the issue of making use of an inappropriate control group with the studies examined here. The problem of making use of an inappropriate control group is a serious one because it raises the issue of the validity of the study findings. In addition, the use of a small sample size in this kind of study leaves considerable room for doubt regarding the generalizability of the findings. We also saw that most of the studies reviewed above identified types of programs studied (academic and/or vocational); however, they did not inform about the length of the programs. Secondly, the issue of "self-selection" of program participants either was acknowledged but not dealt with or not acknowledged at all in the studies examined. Finally, the studies reviewed above also lack qualitative information about the programs investigated.

A REVIEW OF MATISOFF'S 1974 IMPACT ASSESSMENT INVESTIGATION

Martinson published his famous report in 1974. This year was remarkable in the history of correctional education programming in America. Before Martinson's controversial publication, the main correctional philosophy and practice in American was rehabilitative. However, the claim that "nothing works" had considerable impact on the discussion over inmate rehabilitative programs. The rehabilitative philosophy's critics eagerly embraced the "nothing works" report to help justify abandoning rehabilitation and redirecting American correctional philosophy and practice to a greater emphasis on just desert and incapacitation (e.g., Delisi and Conis, 2019; Austin and Irwin, 2001; Gendreau, 1996).

In the same year, Matisoff (1974) published a conclusion somewhat different from that of Martinson. However, Matisoff's report was not as popular as Martinson's, presumably because of the different status of the two authors. Whereas Matisoff's study was a Ph.D. dissertation, Martinson's study was conducted for the New York State Governor's Special Committee on Criminal Offenders, which wanted to know the impact of offender rehabilitation for policy recommendations.

Matisoff (1974) arrived at his conclusions after carrying out a recidivism study of parolees from one of Illinois's Minimum Security Correctional Centers. In his study, Matisoff, obviously aware of some of the earlier studies' weaknesses, addressed the following specific questions:

1. Is there a significant difference between the average recidivism rates for those inmates who participated in the correctional program as compared to those who did not participate?
2. Does the type of program, academic or vocational, lend itself to a lower recidivism rate?
3. Does the number of months of participation in the program produce any significant effect upon the recidivism rate?

4. Does the educational level of the inmate at the time he entered prison have any effect on the recidivism rate, given knowledge of the type of program and number of months of participation?
5. Does the educational program have any significant effect on the length of release-time success?

The subjects of the study consisted of 605 inmates discharged or paroled from the Vienna Correctional Center, Illinois. The criterion group was composed of 445 men (or 73 percent of all discharged inmates) who participated in some kind of educational program delivered at the Center. The control group was made up of 164 men (27 percent of all inmates discharged) of non-school attenders. The period of parole behavior investigation was three years.

Matisoff reported mixed results. First, he found that there were statistically significant differences between: (1) the average recidivism rates for participation and nonparticipation in the education programs. This difference was significant at the .03 level; (2) the difference in average recidivism rates between participants in the vocational program and those who participated in the academic program was statistically significant at the .02 level. Second, he found, however, that there were no statistically significant differences emerging from: (1) comparisons based upon the interaction of the type of program with the number of months of participation; (2) comparison of the educational level of the inmate when he entered Vienna and the number of months of participation in the academic or vocational program.

The results of this correctional education study were published the same year Martinson reported that "nothing works" and in conjunction with the investigations reviewed above seem to warrant correctional education's exception from this blanket indictment.

The strength of Matisoff's evaluation rests on: (a) the use of a large suitable comparison group—criterion and control groups, respectively, were selected by matching variables such as prior criminal records, age, race, and other attributes; and (b) the determination of the effects of the length of program participation.

The major limitations of the evaluation have to do with: (a) the fact that the Vienna inmates in the period studied probably were not representative of most prison inmates. This is because the study was conducted when the institution and its educational programs were still in their developmental stages. More time should have been allowed to see if retrogression set in. The above problem, to an extent, sets limits to the degree of generalizability of the study's findings; (b) failure to mention the problem of self-selection of program participants. Self-selection bias is a serious problem in the study of these kinds of subjects.

In addition, the study also is guilty of the problem of internally undifferentiated experimental group. This problem was pointed out in some of the studies reviewed above In sum, perhaps, what is most important about Matisoff's conclusion was that its findings were, on the face of it, in direct contradiction to Martinson's famous verdict of "nothing works," because the study showed that some things do work for certain inmates, thus supporting the results of most of the above studies.

A REVIEW OF PRISON-BASED EVALUATIVE TREATMENT STUDIES OF THE LATE 1970S THROUGH THE 1980S

The studies reviewed in this section and the subsequent section can be considered responses to previous research, i.e., addressing issues that were raised and examining ones that were not. The first of these studies was conducted in 1981 by Anderson, who carried out an in-depth analysis of the relationship between correctional education and parole success. The research population consisted of a random selection of 400 post-release inmates from a minimum security institution in Illinois. The subjects were subdivided into a criterion group of male parolees who had received vocational training and/or academic education and a control group of male inmates who had obtained neither. Anderson utilized fourteen criteria to determine the impact of vocational or academic training on post-release success. These criteria are as follows:

1. To determine if the amount of vocational training is related to the number of months working on parole.
2. To determine if a relationship exists between number of arrests on parole and parolees having or not having vocational training.
3. To determine if there is a relationship between the level of vocational training completed and violation of parole.
4. To assess whether the type of vocational training is related to parole violation.
5. To evaluate the relationship between type of vocational training and number of months working on parole.
6. To determine if there is a relationship between parolees having or not having vocational training and number of months working on parole.
7. To determine, for those who received vocational training, if a relationship exists between types of vocational training and initial job placement on parole.

8. To evaluate, for those who received vocational training, the relationship between vocational grade-point average and number of months working on parole.
9. To determine if there is a relationship between number of months working on parole and the interval of time between completion of vocational training and release on parole.
10. To assess the relationship between enrolling or not enrolling in academic course work and violation of parole.
11. To assess the relationship between enrolling or not enrolling in academic course work and the number of months employed while on parole.
12. To determine if there is a relationship between institutional academic training and academic or vocational training taken while on parole.
13. To assess the attitude of employers of vocationally trained Vienna parolees toward those parolees and their vocational preparation.
14. To assess the attitude of vocationally trained Vienna parolees toward the training they received. The parole period used ranged from 1 to 24 months.

Anderson reports that analysis of individual criteria overwhelmingly favored prison school graduates over nongraduates. That is, that prison education was shown to be positively correlated with parole success.

Anderson also reports the following. First, 25 employers of vocationally trained Vienna parolees were successfully interviewed, and in this sample, one out of three trainees was hired in jobs related to their vocational training. Second, the skills and attitudes of trainees were highly rated by employers. Third, employers' responses suggested that some areas of vocational training are more marketable, thus associated with positive post-release employment. However, because of small sample size, no definitive conclusions can be made. Anderson made a very important point, which none of the studies examined above considered. He states that "It could be that many parolees who are motivated to become involved in vocational training are similarly motivated to be good employees, regardless of the initial job placement" (Anderson, 1981; Kim and Clark, 2013; Scott, 2018).

Anderson here presents a causal picture that differs from that drawn by many advocates of rehabilitative programs who assume that lowered propensity to recidivate is an effect of exposure to education (e.g., Matisoff, 1974; Cochran, 1965; Zink, 1962; Fox, 1950; Schnur, 1948). Anderson, in contrast, suggests that the propensity to rehabilitate causes both participation in educational programs and successful parole.

The strength of Anderson's study then rests on the number of parole success criteria utilized, qualitative knowledge of the programs studied, as well as the random selection technique employed in the selection of 50 employers of vocationally trained Vienna parolees and, perhaps more importantly, the acknowledgment of the problems of "self-selection" in the study of these subjects.

The issue of self-selection is very serious because it raises the question of whether participation in the program or the motivation to participate in the program is responsible for the impact on recidivism (see, for example, Kim and Clark, 2013; Scott, 2018; Denney and Tynes, 2021). This author believes generally that the motivation to participate in the program is much more responsible for the impact on recidivism than actual participation in the program. This is because parolees' participation in a postsecondary correctional program does not result in greater readiness not to recidivate to prison. Instead, the increased readiness not to recidivate and the interest in participating in prison education programs are the result of the parolees' decision to do what it takes to bring their lives into order.

Thus, some general restructuring of outlook, perhaps a sort of conversion, may be the main factor in determining whether a previously incarcerated and released offender will recidivate; whether that offender participated in the prison-based postsecondary education or not appears to be more of an indicator of the presence of such a new outlook than its cause. If an offender participated in the correctional education program but has not really decided to "go straight" when released into the larger society that offender would be most likely to go back to the life of crime. On the other hand, if an offender did not participate in postsecondary correctional education programming because of lack of opportunity but had already decided to "go straight," it is more likely that when that offender is released into the larger community he or she would not engage in antisocial behavior.

After all, lack of participation in prison-based college education can mean several things—either the lack of opportunity to get into the program or the lack of willingness to go straight, or both. It is important to keep in mind that lack of opportunity to participate in postsecondary correctional education does not go together with the lack of willingness to go straight. It simply means that the inmate could not participate in the program due to lack of chance to do so, which does mean the lack of determination to change from criminality. In such a case, inmate participation or lack of participation in a postsecondary correctional program is not and cannot be the main determining factor of whether that inmate will recidivate or not when released into the larger community. Instead, having embraced a new attitude toward life is the main determining factor. This is so because even if an inmate had the opportunity to participate in the program but did not want to change from his criminal ways of life, participation by itself would not make any difference on how that inmate would perform when released into the larger society. Other limitations of the study include unclear specification of the number of experimental and control groups utilized, incomplete parole records, and the reluctance of ex-offenders to cooperate.

Blackburn (1981) compared the recidivism rates of inmates who participated in a community college program at the Maryland Minimum Security Correctional Training Center with a matched group of nonparticipants. Blackburn examined the recidivism rates of 378 former inmates as measured by arrests for new crimes or reconfinement for parole violations. Subjects received a score on five variables (age at time of release, date of release, prior record, race, and length of incarceration), which provided the basis for a matching of experimental and control group members. The criterion group consisted of 189 parolees who attended education programs while incarcerated, while the other half were a group of parolees who did not participate at all in the college-level programs.

Blackburn reported that the participants in the college programs had an overall recidivism rate one-third lower than nonparticipants. In comparing the recidivists of the two groups, he noted that there was no significant difference in the length of release time before they recidivated.

The strength of this study lies in the use of a control group matched for each member of the experimental group on the variables noted above. The implementation of this method allowed Blackburn to claim that the "experimental group differed from the control group in a single (measured) respect: program participation." The major limitations of this study were inability to clearly define which group of parolees he referred to as program participants, this being the same problem common to most studies reviewed above. Secondly, the study made no mention of the issue of self-selection, which is common with this kind of study.

Linden et al. (1984) conducted a study comprising two penitentiaries (British Columbia Penitentiary, a maximum security institution, and Matsqui Penitentiary, a medium security prison), in the attempt to evaluate the impact of a prison-based postsecondary education program on recidivism. Interestingly, he made use of a pretest/posttest experimental design. This design seems to represent an improvement over most previous studies of this nature because the results of the posttest would enable the researchers to make a strong claim that participation in a prison-based education program is, to an extent, responsible for any difference of any that might occur in the comparison.

The subject group was made up of 66 inmates in the experimental and control groups respectively. Three years was used as the trial period. The researchers attempted to make sure that the two groups were similar in most respects. To accomplish that they used analysis of variance to determine whether significant differences existed between the groups; basic demographic information about each inmate was examined; previous criminal activities and institutional adjustment were measured. Both groups were selected for the program on a volunteer basis.

Linden et al. reported that the British Columbia participants were more successful than those of Matsqui. This finding is surprising in the sense that most research, as well as theories of prisons such as prisonization theory (Clemmer, 1958; Sykes, 1958), tends to suggest that inmates from medium and minimum security prisons were more suitable candidates for rehabilitation than inmates from maximum security institutions. This is because inmates from medium and minimum security institutions are low-level offenders and often serve fewer years in prison, which means a more limited immersion into the inmate culture, and, finally, the institutions are relatively relaxed because steps are being taken to make the communities look like life outside the wall. The situations in maximum security institutions are just the opposite of those described above. The researchers note that the differences between the experimental and control groups of B.C. Penitentiary were not statistically significant (p .05).

This author believes that the strengths of this research lie in the methodology used. The study's use of pretest and posttest experimental design was a novel approach and represents an improvement over most previous research of this kind.

On the other hand, there are several weaknesses; for instance, the report noted (on p.71) that the majority of the Matsqui group were drug addicts. It is well documented that drug addicts have a very high recidivism rate (e.g., Vandala, 2019). It could be that it was this criminogenic lifestyle that led to the recidivism differences between the two groups. Another weakness of the study could be the fact that a small number of inmates were involved in the study, which meant that differences of this size could have occurred by chance.

In addition, five months of schooling was the length of the programs, which is a short period of time for any educational program, particularly for students who have extensive educational deficiencies and who require a great deal of remedial help. Finally, and perhaps more importantly, the population for this study were self-selected, which raises the question of whether participation in the program or the motivation to participate in the program is responsible for the impact on recidivism. This author reaffirms that the motivation to participate in these kinds of program is probably more responsible for the impact on recidivism than the actual participation in the program.

Holloway and Moke (1986) carried out a one-year follow-up study of parolees to determine if participation in college education affected their post-release behavior in terms of employment, arrest, and returning to prison. An experimental group of 95 inmates who received associate degrees was compared with two groups: a quasi-control group of 116 offenders who received high school degrees and 106 inmates who were high school dropouts.

They found that the college graduates did not exhibit statistically significant higher performance on the variables mentioned above. They noted, however, that the absence of statistically significant relationships between educational attainment, employment, arrest, and recidivism among college graduates is not necessarily conclusive, due to the small number of parolees who recidivated from all three groups.

This study is not exhaustive. The small number of parolees available for this study, as well as the relatively short period of time the parolees spent on parole, render the measures of success/failure of the study not very trustworthy. It is imperative to make sure that a relatively large number of parolees are included in this kind of study and to allow a relatively long period for the parolees to spend on parole before their assessment. Two years is usually regarded as enough time to measure parole success/failure because most parolees who are likely to recidivate do so within this time frame (Anderson, 1981; Robinson, 1990; Scott, 2018).

Lessons Learned from the Studies of 1980s

It is obvious that the studies of the 1980s attempted to address some of the substantive and methodological issues left unaddressed by previous studies on the subjects. Indeed, the studies of the 1980s show some improvement in the methods used, yet they have a few other methodological flaws that need to be addressed. These problems may create doubts about the findings of the studies.

The studies of the 1980s also show some improvement in the substantive nature of the research, yet they left some important issues unacknowledged or mentioned them in passing. Some of these issues include: the problems of self-selection, the length of the education programs, exactly what is it about education program that presumably reduces offender recidivism. How long does program participation have to last for the educational impact to sink in? It is important that future researchers on this subject take note of these issues and flaws and try to minimize them as much as possible.

The studies of the 1980s addressed Martinson's "nothing works" conclusion and provided evidence by supporting the idealistic position on offender rehabilitation instead of Martinson's pessimism. However, it is important to point out that the 1980s studies reviewed focused specifically on prison-based education programs. These programs are only one form of offender rehabilitation efforts, whereas Martinson reviewed several, if not all, forms of offender rehabilitation program literature.

A REVIEW OF PRISON-BASED EDUCATION IMPACT ASSESSMENT OF THE 1990S

The first research of the 1990s studies to be examined was conducted by Langenbach et al. (1990). Langenbach and his colleagues carried out a corrections education impact analysis study of Oklahoma medium and minimum security institutions for the purpose of investigating two questions: (1) Is there a relationship between participation in college course work and subsequent reincarceration rates? And (2) are there changes in the frequency of disciplinary actions prior to, during, or after participation in Televised Instructional System (TIS) while incarcerated?

To stay within the framework of this study, we shall focus on the first question addressed in the Langenbach et al. (1990) study. This means that only the findings relating to the first question of their study will be provided in this analysis.

The total population of the study consisted of 733 inmates, out of which the criterion group is made up of 373 inmates, whereas the comparison is 360 inmates. The experimental group is a group of inmates that participated in college-level courses via a televised instructional system (TIS), whereas 360 inmates composed the matched control group of nonparticipants in the TIS. This matched group was restricted to inmates released since December 1979, the month of the first release of TIS participants. The group was matched based on the following variables: offender age, race, offense group, length of sentence, and facility/location.

Langenbach et al. found that a significant positive relationship exists between participation in TIS and reduction in recidivism. The difference in recidivism rate between parolees who participated in TIS and nonparticipants was statistically significant at the .01 level.

The strengths of this study rest on its methodology, i.e., the use of a reasonably large study population in both the experimental and the control groups. Although the study subjects were not randomly selected, the matching method is regarded as second best to randomization (which often is not possible in this kind of research), and as such, the matching technique should be seen as a strength of the study.

A weakness of the study, as the researchers later noted, involves two demographic variables not available on the automated system. These variables were self-reported employment history and level of schooling. Although information shows that more participants than nonparticipants were employed before the time they recidivated than nonparticipants, and that participants had a higher level of schooling than the nonparticipants, causal inferences regarding participation and recidivism cannot be made for sure. It may be that both participation in TIS and parole success were simply manifestation of some other underlying differences among inmates. A closer look will be given to this possibility in the discussion of the findings of the following study by Robinson.

Robinson (1990) carried out a study to clarify the effect of participation in educational programs on post-release recidivism of paroled inmates. He compared the post-release behavior of Missouri parolees from medium and minimum institutions who completed either academic or vocational correctional programs with that of noncompleters. The data for the study consisted of 599 inmates of school attendants (completers and noncompleters). The determination was assessed over a period of four years.

Robinson found that there were no significant relationships between recidivism after one year, two years, three years, or four years of parole and participation in the college or vocational program. However, findings show that there was a pattern of parolees who participated in the college or vocational program and completed the training to recidivate at a lower rate than those parolees who had participated in the college or vocational program but did not complete the training.

This author thinks that the strength of this research lies in the large number of subjects studied. This number is large enough to allow the results of the study to be generalized to a wider inmate population. The limitations of the study include the fact that the study fails to acknowledge the problems of self-selection endemic in this kind of research. The study also failed to point out the length of each of the programs studied nor did it give a somewhat systematic account of what exactly it is about an education program that is supposed to reduce offender recidivism. In addition, the study falls short of making a comprehensive impact assessment that involves program completers, noncompleters, and nonprogram participants. Studies that will make such a comprehensive impact analysis are needed because such studies would enable us to have a complete knowledge of the difference, if any, among the above program categories.

Schumacker et al. (1990) conducted a substantial study to assess whether vocational training in prison has effects on inmates' post-release behavior in terms of employment and parole success. A comparison was carried out between releasees who have only vocational training, a mix of vocational/academic training, and a group of releasees who did not have any training at all. The next group studied were those releasees who received only academic but no vocational course work while incarcerated. The total number of subjects studied was 760, provided by 19 adult correctional institutions in midwestern states. The study covered a period of 12 months.

Schumacker et al. found that the vocational and vocational/academic groups combined had the highest employment rates, lower combined unemployment rates, and lower criminal activity rates. The comparison group had the highest criminal activity rates. When those who graduated from vocational training were compared with nonvocational graduates, the vocational graduates still had higher employment and fewer arrests than the control group. The academic group, however, had the lowest employment rate and second highest criminal activity rate.

This study has major strengths, which include the substantial number of subjects studied, coupled with the several criterion and control groups compared. In addition, the results of this study are probably generalizable to the general inmate population mainly because its sample was drawn from 19 adult correctional institutions in the midwestern states. A limitation of this study is the failure of the researchers to separate the program group, referred to as nonvocational graduates. This is because nonvocational graduates encompass two program groups—nonvocational completers and nonvocational participants. These categories need to be separated in the study of these subjects.

O'Neil (1990) engaged in a study of correctional educational programming in a minimum- security correctional institution in Alabama to answer the major question: Is there a significant relationship between participation in postsecondary correctional education and lower rates of recidivism? 129 postsecondary schooling participants were compared to the same number of nonparticipants chosen through random selection. The determination period for the parole success was one year. Results indicate a statistically significant relationship at the .05 level between participation in correctional PSE and rates of recidivism. Of the general population studied, 7.7 percent were recidivists. Of the 7.7 percent who became recidivists, about two-thirds had not participated in postsecondary correctional education programming and one-third had been active in the PSE program.

The major strength of this study rests on the use of the random selection method to sample the study population. Random selection is the best sampling method in this kind of research. As far as the generalizability of the results of the study is concerned, the small number of subjects studied could be regarded as the limitation of this evaluation. The undifferentiated experimental group is also a limitation of this study. Finally, the study did not mention the type of correctional educational program studied (academic or vocational or both) nor acknowledge the issue of self-selection of program participants—a serious problem in these kinds of subjects (e.g., Denney and Tynes, 2021). In the same vein as some studies examined above, Wilson (1994) assessed the impact of vocational correctional education on the recidivism rate of adjudicated youth in Colorado. He compared 260 youths who received vocational training with 143 youths with no vocational training. A five-year follow-up was the trial period.

Wilson found that 159 out of the 260 youths who received some vocational training while at the Division of Youth Services were incarcerated in an adult corrections facility. The recidivism rate of 143 youths with no vocational training was 78.3 percent—17 percent higher than the recidivism rate of 61.2 percent of youths who received vocational training. Wilson concludes that there is a significant difference between the recidivism rates of vocationally and nonvocationally trained youths.

Although the trial period (five years) used was long enough to enable assessment of the impact of vocational education on recidivism, this study can be charged as limited because of its failure to specify the program category or categories that made up the experimental group. This is because correctional vocational participants could mean a combination of vocational completers and noncompleters. In addition, this study did not tell how the youth who participated in vocational training were drafted or how long the program took, nor make the case of the issue of self-selection. Also, there was no qualitative data concerning the programs studied.

Jenkins et al. (1995), in a follow-up study of correctional vocational education program participants of minimum and medium security institutions in Maryland, evaluated inmates who completed vocational educational training while in prison to assess the impact of their training in obtaining employment upon release. The total of 120 educational completers was compared with noneducational completers in the general inmate population. A one-year post-release was used as a trial period. The demographic and criminal justice variables of the two groups were similar. The only major difference between the groups was in terms of race, with 59 percent of the study group and 76 percent of the general prison population being nonwhite. Jenkins et al. assert that there is a positive relationship between education attainment while incarcerated and later success in the community.

The strength of this study lies in the similarity of the demographic and criminal justice variables of both the inmates in the study group and those in the general prison population. If that was the case, it suggests that the study's findings are generalizable to the general inmate population. On the other hand, the study fails to point out the length of the programs studied and, above all, the issue of self-selection known to affect the impact of the programs.

Lessons Learned from the Studies of the 1990s

In sum, it can be concluded that the studies of the 1990s reviewed here systematically responded to the methodological issues raised by previous studies on the subjects but, on the other hand, did not do the same to the substantive issues they raised. This is so because a careful assessment of the literature of the 1990s studies on the subject shows increased methodological rigor but little substantive progress. Thus, the methods utilized by researchers of the 1990s are a lot more sophisticated than those of earlier time periods. For example, studies of the 1990s made use of larger study populations and better measurements of recidivism, such as reinstitutionalization into a correctional institution, than their earlier counterparts. However, just as in the other time periods, studies of the 1990s also have flaws of their own such as the use of undifferentiated experimental groups and a weak control group, and above all, they did not describe the programs they studied well enough.

We also learned that the results of the 1990s studies seem to challenge the famous "nothing works" conclusion by Martinson, in the sense that they overwhelmingly support the idealistic position which suggests that exposure to correctional education program have the propensity to make a difference in the recidivism rates of parolees. Thus, all but one of the studies of the 1990s show a positive significant association between participation and/or completion of correctional education and recidivism. Yet, it cannot be said that studies of the 1990s made noticeable advances in the understanding of the interacting causal patterns underlying the statistical association between correctional education and recidivism. While the crucial issue of potential self-selection bias was mentioned by several studies of the 1990s, none seriously attempted to tackle the problem in a way that is critical and deep enough. The results of the studies of the 1990s reviewed above seem to suggest at least three things: that participation in correctional education programs is associated with offenders' positive rehabilitative effects on recidivism; that the association between correctional education and recidivism is sufficiently robust to show up regardless of the methods used; and that the crucial issue of the causes of this association is not nearly as carefully addressed as one might expect.

A REVIEW OF PRISON-BASED TREATMENT PROGRAMS IMPACT ASSESSMENT OF 2000–2010

The first study of the 2000–2010 period that meets the criteria used for the selection of studies for review in this book was conducted by Kelso (2000). Kelso studied the overall Washington State recidivism rates as compared to the rates of two specific education programs in the same state. Specifically, the data for the study included the recidivism rates of all Washington State Department of Corrections (WSDOC) inmates of 7,856 population released from the state correctional institution between 1985–1987 and were tracked for a five-year period. A replication of recidivism data of the same study period, as well as five-year tracking period of releases of inmates utilized in the WSDOC study, also was used in the replication study focusing specifically on two institutions in the state: the Garrett Haynes Correctional Center (GHEC) and the Twin Rivers Correctional Center (TRCC) recidivism rates respectively. These two programs included vocational and college inmate education graduates except GED certificate recipients. The return of a previously released inmate to Washington State Correctional Facility because of a new felony conviction or technical violation, or both, was used as the measurement of recidivism.

Comparisons of the studies' results indicate that the recidivism rates of both the GHEC and the TRCC were much better than those of the overall WSDOC at statistically significant levels. Specifically, the Washington Department of Corrections overall average recidivism rate was 30.9 percent, the GHEC was 14.3 percent, and that of the TRCC group was 10.8 percent. The average recidivism rates difference between the study groups of WSDOC and GHEC was 53.7 percent reduction in favor of the GHEC groups, whereas the difference between the WSDOC and TRCC study groups was 65 percent reduction. The results of these studies are consistent with the widely held notion that participation in postsecondary correctional education makes a significant difference when compared with the recidivism rates of group of inmates who did not participate. That is, the higher the level of education attainment, the greater the chances of success upon released from prison.

Several strengths can be credited to this study. Among them are the fact that the study utilizes a diverse set of data of large inmate population from four different states. This diverse set of data has greater likelihood to strengthen the generalizability of the result findings to the general inmate population. Another strength of the study is the use of five years as the recidivism measurement period, in that it is a very significant window of measurement of recidivism because research has shown that most recidivism occurs within the first two years of release from prison. Using a window of five years as a measurement of risks of recidivism is a stretch because this duration of assessment is hardly used in similar studies. Perhaps some credit also should be given to this study for acknowledging the issue of self-selection bias which usually affects most studies of this nature. Having recognized the issue as a major problem, the study creatively puts it in perspective in a way that is persuasive.

However, there are some weaknesses in the study. First among them is that it does not disclose how much time program graduates with diplomas, degrees, and vocational certificates spent in their respective programs to enable us to be aware of their duration, which is important information for assessment of the quality of the programs. In addition, this study did not discuss the security levels of the institutions studied. Knowledge of this information can be very important as it would enable a better understanding of the idiosyncrasies of what works between correctional education program and recidivism in relation to the security levels of the correctional institutions the data came from. This is so because correctional institutions vary in their security levels, and different correctional security-level institutions usually hold different types of offenders, and some security-level institutions are more amenable for successful offender rehabilitation and reintegration than others. As such, the information can be a valuable tool in the analysis of the relationship between correctional education and recidivism.

Burke and Vivian (2001) analyzed the effect of college programming on recidivism rates of parolees from the Hampden County Correctional Center in Ludlow, Massachusetts. The study group consisted of 32 ex-inmates who had college experience while at the facility and a corresponding comparison group of 32 parolees who did not. Five years post-release measure was used as the examination period of recidivism for parolees who were later reincarcerated into the Hampden County Correctional Facility and those who were not.

Results indicate that in the five-year period studied, differences in post-release criminality existed, favoring the college group members. The differences of the success rate were statistically significant at the 22 percent level of confidence in favor of the college participants. Findings also indicate that there was a longer length of time for those inmates who participated in prison-based college education than those who did not, with the average length of 4.38 years compared with 3.13 years.

This study has some major strengths, which include that the two comparison groups are demographically similar in age, education level upon incarceration, sentence length, gender, and ethnicity. Controlling these variables between the two groups studied helps a great deal in reducing the differences that might have existed between the groups before comparison. The five-year investigation period used was a real strength because the period was long enough to enable assessment of the impact of postsecondary education on recidivism. It was also enough to see if retrogression will set in. Another strength of the study involves its definition of recidivism. In contrast to most studies on the subject, which make use of arrest and/or conviction as an indicator of recidivism, this study makes use of resentencing to a prison as a measure of recidivism. This author thinks that this measure of recidivism is a more appropriate and acceptable indicator, especially when we are dealing with reincarceration which encompasses "a return to prison" (Duwe, 2019; Steven and Ward, 1997; Meiser, 1989). This is so because not all parolees arrested and/or convicted do return to prison. Perhaps, a more important strength of this study is the acknowledgment of the problems of "self-selection" in the study of these subjects. As I have stressed elsewhere, the issue of self-selection is a very serious one because it raises the question of whether actual participation in the program or the motivation to participate in the program and/or the willingness to do what it takes to “go straight” from the life of crime is responsible for the impact on recidivism.

On the other hand, it can be said that the study is limited in some respects, the first among them being the failure of the researchers to separate the program group referred to as college group. This is because college group encompasses two groups—college completers and non-college completers. These categories of college groups need to be separated in the study of these subjects. This is because such a separation would enable us to have better knowledge and insight as to the differences, if any, that exist between the two program groups’ recidivism rates. This knowledge is important for correctional policy and practice. Another limitation of the research lies in the small number of subjects studied. This number is so small as to raise the question of whether the result of the study is easily generalizable to the general inmate population. As suggested by literature on the subject, a sample size below 100 is often viewed as unreliable (Hall, 2015).

In another impact assessment study, Steurer et al. (2001) investigated whether participation in a correctional education program while incarcerated reduces the risk of recidivism for inmates who reentered into the general communities. A quasi-experimental group consisting of 1373 inmates who participated in prison-based education was compared to a control group of 1797 inmates with no school attendance. In the attempts to generate a broad based of release cohort of parolees for the study, the authors made use of the entire population of inmates that were released within a specific period rather than a sampling of group from the entire parole population. This assessment was done in three states—Maryland, Minnesota, and Ohia. The three commonly used forms of measurement of recidivism in scholarly literature for this kind of subject were utilized—rearrest, reconviction, and reincarceration. Three years follow-up was used as the measurement period for the study. The result findings of the study indicate that simply attending school behind bars reduces the likelihood of reincarceration by 29 percent.

This author thinks that a major strength of this study has to do with the fact that the study was conducted with a data set from three different states’ correctional agencies with a total study population of 3170 parolees. The fact that the study population was generated from those three states’ offender population, and the findings indicate recidivism results that were similar among the three states’ studies, clearly suggests that the result of the study is generalizable to the general parole population. However, some weaknesses can also be attributed to this study. For example, the study did not disclose the security levels of the correctional institutions. It also failed to clearly separate the major education groups studied. As I have stressed previously in this manuscript, the information about the security levels of correctional agencies, as well as the education levels of the program parolees participated in while in prison, ought to be made clear for systematic and critical examination and analysis.

The use of rearrest, reconviction, and reinstitutionalization in measuring recidivism in one study like this one may be viewed as a weakness in the sense that the use of those three measurements at the same time may lead to misunderstanding and misinterpretation of the true nature of the results' findings of a study. This is so because the implications of the nature and differing recidivism rates of the three measurements of recidivism usually vary from one another. As research has shown, the use of rearrest and reconviction as measurements of recidivism usually produces greater recidivism rates than the use of reinstitutionalization. For example, a comprehensive recidivism study among federal offenders conducted by the United States Sentencing Commission (2016), in which the three measures of recidivism—rearrest, reconviction, and reinstitutionalized—were utilized show differing recidivism rates among them (i.e., 49.3 percent were rearrested, 31.7 percent were reconvicted, and 24.6 percent were reinstitutionalized). This observed lower recidivism rate outcome measure with the use of reinstitutionalization has more to do with the fact that the measure has more exhaustive steps in its process than the other two measures. This is so because for an offender to be reinstitutionalized back to prison, that offender must first be rearrested and reconvicted. And this is a major attribute of reinstitutionalization, which gives it greater appeal and acceptability than rearrest and reconviction as the most effective, reliable, and credible indicator of recidivism (e.g., Delisi and Conis, 2019; Berghuis, 2018; Scott, 2018; Kim and Clark, 2013; Chappell, 2004; Ubah, 2002).

Lipsey and Cullen (2007) carried out a meta-analysis of meta-analyses studies to determine what is known about the effectiveness of correctional sanction, supervision, and rehabilitation treatments on offender recidivism. In keeping with the focus of this book, this review only focuses on the effects of rehabilitation treatment on offender recidivism aspects of the systematic analysis. To be clear, a meta-analysis study is a systematic quantitative form of research synthesis that involves statistical effect sizes formulated to represent the difference in outcomes between intervention and control groups across multiple studies (Cooper, 1998; Lipsey and Cullen, 2007).

The researchers reviewed dozens of meta-analysis studies that have been conducted with the purpose of comparing the recidivism rates of offenders who participated in prison-based correctional education program with a substantially similar control group of offenders who did not participate so that informed determination can be made as to whether participation in a prison-based correctional program is effective or not in reducing recidivism. Lipsey and Cullen (2007) found near universal results of effectiveness of the prison-based rehabilitation programs included in the meta-analysis study.

That is, results of every one of the meta-analyses studies examined show that participation in a correctional rehabilitation program while incarcerated were effective as compared to nonparticipants.

Perhaps, the main strength of this study lies in the fact that it was a meta-analysis of dozens of meta-analyses that examined many empirical studies on offender rehabilitation programs, which thereby offer us the opportunity to be aware and appreciate the broad view of the current state of effectiveness of prison-based correctional rehabilitation programs in reducing offender recidivism. On the other hand, some number of weaknesses can be attributed to this study. A striking one among them may have to do with its result findings, in the sense that a well-known potential bias of meta-analyses of published studies is the tendency for them to show greater positive effect sizes than nonpublished ones because of various reasons which presumably include the selection processes associated with the development, submission, and review of literatures for journal publication (Nally et al., 2012; Rothstein et al., 2005). However, whether this possibility applies or not to the results of the meta-analysis studies examined in this study is not clear because the result of the findings of the unpublished studies included in the meta-analyses also indicate positive findings in the same direction as the published ones included in the studies. Therefore, it is important that future studies on the subject investigate the issue more deeply with the aim of sharing more lessons and insights on it.

Winterfield et al. (2009) conducted an inmate evaluation study with the goal of exploring the motivations for participating in postsecondary correctional education, the impact of postsecondary education on prison inmates, and the expected effects or lack of them of postsecondary correctional education after release from prison custody. The study utilized qualitative and quantitative observational data from minimum- and medium-level security institutions that offer postsecondary education programs in three states—Indiana, Massachusetts, and New Mexico. The current inmate enrollment in postsecondary education during the period of the study in the three states were Indiana with 2700 enrollments; Massachusetts with a little over 180 enrollments; and New Mexico with 647 enrollments.

The researchers reported that both inmates and stakeholders were enthusiastic about postsecondary education in each of the state facilities studied. Consistent themes across respondents and study sites were that postsecondary education had a positive impact on inmate behavior; that participation in the program increased their self-esteem and their employment prospects and thereby increasing their chances of making a successful transition upon release into the general society. Analysis of post-release recidivism rates of inmates who participated in a postsecondary education program as compared to those who did not show that participation had a substantial and statistically significant success rate across study locations compared to nonparticipants.

Several strengths can be attributed to this study. Among them include the fact that the study made use of large data set from three states—Indiana, Massachusetts, and New Mexico. This diverse group of study population from several correctional institutions with different offender population increases the generalizability of the result findings greatly to the general inmate population. By utilizing quantitative and qualitative research methods, the study offers an opportunity for audience awareness of some of the various interacting variables at work in the study. Even though the issue of weak research design still exists with the study, as illustrated below, some credit should probably be given to the study, in that, unlike most studies on the subject that do not recognize the potential problem of self-selection bias, this study takes some reasonable steps by utilizing a boosted regression method along with inverse probability weighting to minimize the problem.

Yet, when all is said and done, there is no other research design out there that is better than a randomize method of selection of subjects for a study of this kind and this study did not utilize that. The study also had some missing data on some measures for some large number of subjects studied, which if the measures were available probably could have produced some information that may provide some important lessons and help shed some deeper insights on the overall character of the study.

Perhaps, another issue worth pointing out about the study is that there wasn't a unified definition of recidivism utilized in the post-release outcomes of the three states studied, but instead, differing measures of recidivism were used. This is so because, while Indiana defined recidivism as a return to prison for any reason, including technical violation, Massachusetts and New Mexico define it as a new arrest either for any offences or technical violation. These are two distinct definitions of recidivism that could easily lead to significant differences at the rates at which reentry prisoners could return to prison. This is so because, as we know, anyone could easily be arrested for one reason or another by a police officer, and sometimes those arrests may be dismissed rather quickly because of various reasons including lack of establishment of any infraction or offense of any sort. In such a case, using arrest as an indicator of recidivism may be misleading at best. On the other hand, using "a return to prison" as an indicator of recidivism offers a more credible and acceptable measure, in that the measure means that a returning offender has been rearrested, reconvicted, and reinstitutionalized in the custody of a correctional institution, either because of committing a new offense or because of a technical violation, or both. As a result, this measure seems to offer a more appropriate and acceptable indicator of recidivism than rearrest and/or reconviction (e.g., Delisi and Conis, 2019; Scott, 2018; Kim and Clark, 2013; Ubah, 2002).

Lessons Learned from the Studies of 2000–2010

Several lessons can be gleaned from the studies of 2000–2010 examined above. A careful reading of the literature interestingly shows that there are some similarities as well as distinctions between the 2000–2010 studies and that of the1990s. For instance, just like the studies of the 1990s, the studies of 2000–2010 systematically responded to the methodological issues raised by previous studies on the subjects. This is so because a careful assessment of the literature of the 2000–2010 studies on the subject shows increased methodological rigor. Thus, the methods utilized by researchers of the 2000–2010 studies are a lot more sophisticated than those of earlier time periods. For example, studies of the 2000–2010 period made use of larger study populations than their earlier counterparts. However, just as in the other time periods, studies of 2000–2010 also have flaws of their own such as the use of some undifferentiated experimental groups and a weak control group and did not describe some of the programs they studied well enough.

As was the case with the results of the 1990s studies, the results of the 2000–2010 studies seem to challenge the famous "nothing works" conclusion by Martinson (1974) in the sense that they overwhelmingly support the idealistic position which suggests that exposure to a correctional education program have the propensity to make a difference in the recidivism rates of parolees. They findings of the studies of 2000–2010 were so conclusive in their results that all the studies examined for the period show a positive significant association between participation and/or completion of correctional education and recidivism. As such, it can be said to a certain degree of conviction that studies of 2000–2010 made significant advances in the understanding of the interacting causal patterns underlying the statistical association between correctional education and recidivism. This is so because not only did the studies recognize the crucial issue of self-selection bias in the study of these kinds of subjects but also took noticeable steps to seriously tackle the problem so that it can be controlled to a significant extent. Like the results of the studies of the 1990s, those of 2000–2010 seem to suggest at least three things: that participation in correctional education programs is associated with offenders' positive rehabilitative effects on recidivism; and that the association between correctional education and recidivism is sufficiently robust to show up regardless of the methods used. In contrast to the studies of 1990s, however, the studies of 2000–2010 seem to make serious attempts to address the potential problem of self-selection bias, which is a crucial issue with the study of these kinds of subjects.

In measuring recidivism, some studies of 2000–2010 made use of arrest and/or conviction as an indicator of recidivism. This book has not hesitated in its view that these indicators of recidivism are problematic, especially when we are dealing with reincarceration. This is so because, with respect to incarceration, the definition of recidivism encompasses “a return to prison.” However, not all parolees rearrested and/or reconvicted do really return to prison. Therefore, reinstitutionalization into a correctional institution as a measure of recidivism appears to be a more credible, appropriate, and acceptable indicator (Denney and Tynes, 2021; Scott, 2018; Chappell, 2004; Ubah, 2002; Steven and Ward, 1997; Meiser, 1989). This measure means that the ex-inmate has been rearrested, processed, reconvicted, and reincarcerated into the custody of a correctional institution (state or federal), either because of a technical violation or because of committing a new crime, or both. Based on this well-established fact, it is appropriate that future studies on the subject make use of reinstitutionalization as an indicator of recidivism instead of rearrest and/or reconviction.

A REVIEW OF PRISON-BASED REHABILITATION PROGRAMS IMPACT ASSESSMENT OF 2011–2022

The first prison-based rehabilitation programs impact assessment study of 2011–2022 to be reviewed here was conducted by Nally et al. (2012). The researchers carried out a five-year (2005–2009) fellow-up study to explore the impact or lack of it of prison inmates’ education and post-release employment on recidivism among different types of offenders (i.e., violent, nonviolent, sex, and drug offenders) with different level of education (i.e., below high school, high school, and two year or above college diploma). The study population consisted of a cohort of 6,561 offenders released from Indiana Department of Corrections (IDOC) in 2005. This data set came from three primary data sources. They are: (1) IDOC Division of Research and Planning; (2) IDOC Education Division; and (3) Indiana Department of Workforce Development (DWD). The study utilized reinstitutionalization back to IDOC custody either because of a parole technical violation or committing a new criminal offense, or both, as the measure of recidivism rates.

The findings of the study revealed that in each of the offender types evaluated, the offenders with college education performed significantly better on post-release employment and recidivism and on other contributing factors to post-release recidivism (age, race, gender, and duration of employment). The results of this study with those of 2000–2010 because it seems to lend support to the idea that provision of postsecondary correctional education and inmate participation in it could not only enable inmates to gain legitimate employment after release from prison but also could enable them not to return to prison as recidivists. In other words, the programs could serve as "hooks" that mediate against criminogenic needs for the best interest of the offender and his/her immediate and extended communities.

This study has a few clearly identifiable strengths. Among them are that the study makes use of the large data set that was generated from three primary sources: (1) IDOC Division of Research and Planning; (2) IDOC Education Division; and (3) Indiana Department of Workforce Development (DWD). This author thinks that this is a very important strength of the study because the information gathered from each of these three primary sources of data for the study feeds and blends on one another and, as a result, fills the lapses and/or gaps that could have occurred had the data set came from just one source. Therefore, the use of information from those various sources enriched as well as strengthened the overall strengths and quality of the collective data set of the study.

Also, the fact that the data set was large enough increases the generalizability of the findings of the study to the general inmate population. Another strength of the study is that it utilizes reinstitutionalization as an outcome measure of recidivism. As has been emphasized repeatedly in this book, reinstitutionalization as an indicator of recidivism appears to be a more exhaustive, credible, and highly appropriate measure of recidivism than rearrest and/or reconviction. This is because reinstitutionalization measure means that a returning offender has been rearrested, reconvicted, and reinstitutionalized in the custody of IDOC either because of committing a new offense or because of a technical violation, or both. Even though it cannot be said for sure that any study, including this one, is perfect in all aspects, this author had a hard time figuring out some well-established research-based reasonable weaknesses of this study.

Kim and Clark (2013) conducted an impact assessment study consisting of a treatment group of 340 and a comparison group of 680 with the primary purpose of ascertaining the true treatment effect of prison-based postsecondary education on recidivism. To that end, the study embarked on two objectives. First, it utilized Propensity Score Matching (PSM) research method to constitute a matched comparison group designed to eliminate the effects of self-selection bias. To be clear, Propensity Score Matching (PSM) is a research method that identifies a similar group of individuals who are not in the treatment group. Such group of individuals becomes a counterfactual for the treatment group and makes it possible to determine what could have happened to the treatment group without exposure to treatment. Second, to ascertain the effects of prison-based postsecondary education on recidivism, the study utilized a fixed-effects logistic regression to measure the recidivism of those prisoners who completed prison-based postsecondary education.

Rearrest was utilized as an indicator of recidivism and three years on parole was used as the measurement period.

The results of the study show that released prisoners who completed prison-based college education programs while in prison recidivated at a lower rate than a PSM-derived comparison group of released prisoners at the rate of 9.4 percent and 17.1 percent respectively. Whereas, when the released prisoners who completed prison-based college education programs while in prison were compared with a comparison group not derived with PSM method, the recidivate rate of the non-PSM group was double that of the matched. The results of this study support the notion that self-selection bias could be a potential problem in the study of the treatment effects of these kinds of subjects, especially when such potential bias was not taken to account and appropriate measures applied to compensate for that bias. In such a situation an inflated estimate of the treatment effect could occur (e.g., Denney and Tynes, 2021; Fogarty and Giles, 2018; Duwe, 2017; Robinson, 1981). The results of this study are clearly in agreement with a growing number of recent studies on the subject.

Several more strengths can be accredited to this study. Perhaps, the most important among them was the use of PSM to establish the comparison group so that the potential inflation of the treatment effect emulating from self-selection bias can be minimized significantly. This is evident with the differential recidivism rates of a comparison group derived with PSM technique and the one that was formulated without the technique. This is a very important strength of the study as it shows that when the potential problem of self-selection bias in this kind of study was not taken into account and appropriate measures applied to compensate for it, inflated treatment effect could occur (e.g., Muhlhausen and Hurwitz, 2019).

This author thinks that a major weakness of the study worthy of mentioning is that it utilizes rearrest as a measure of recidivism. The use of rearrest as an indicator of recidivism may be misleading at best. This is because, as we know with the workings of the criminal justice system, anyone could easily be arrested and rearrested for one reason or the other by police officers, and sometimes those arrests may be dismissed rather quickly for various reasons, including lack of merits before the court of law. Therefore, using rearrest as an indicator of recidivism is problematic as it could be misleading. As a result, instead of using "rearrest" as an indicator of recidivism, we should rather use "a return to prison." This is because "a return to prison" as a measure of recidivism appears to offer a more exhaustive and highly credible measure than rearrest. That is so because the measure means that a returning offender has been rearrested, reconvicted, and reinstitutionalized into the custody of a correctional institution, either by committing a new offense or because of a technical violation, or both. In such a case, this measure seems to offer a more exhaustive, highly appropriate, and acceptable indicator of recidivism than rearrest and/or reconviction (e.g., Delisi and Conis, 2019; Berghuis, 2018; Scott, 2018; Duwe, 2017; Kim and Clark, 2013; Ubah, 2002).

Davis et al. (2013) carried out a meta-analysis of 50 studies that investigated the effects of correctional education programs on recidivism. The researchers examined combined 71 effect size estimates from the 50 studies. The programs investigated include Adult Basic Education, GED, and postsecondary education including college courses and vocational training. The researchers explored whether the relationship between correctional education and recidivism varies by program types and instructional delivery methods as well as group of studies that seemed to have more rigorous research design. The majority of the 50 studies the researchers investigated made use of reincarceration as an outcome measure of recidivism and one and three years after release from prison as a follow-up at risk period of recidivism.

Findings of the study show strong and clear evidence of large and statistically significant reduction of the risk of recidivism following participation in both the basic education correctional programs and postsecondary correctional programs. This result supports those found in a body of recent studies on the subject that indicate that participation in prison-based education has a significant reduction on recidivism rates (e.g., Denney and Tynes, 2021; Pelletier and Evans, 2019; Evans, 2018; Fogarty and Giles, 2018: Pompoco et al., 2017; Karpowitz, 2017; Hall, 2015; Ginsberg, 2014; Lewen, 2014; Davis et al., 2013; Kim and Clark, 2013; Steurer et al., 2010; Brazell et al., 2009). However, the result of reduction of the risks of recidivism following participation in vocation education programs was less clear, which suggests that there may be many low power studies in the programs that have a tendency for statistically significant results to be outlier observations and for the vocational education programs estimate to be relatively imprecise (Fogarty and Giles, 2018; Scott, 2018; Ioannidis et al., 2017; Caudy et al. 2016; Stanley and Doucouliagos, 2014). This finding contrasts with an array of studies on the subject that show that participation in vocational education programs have a clear positive effect on recidivism when compared with nonparticipants (e.g., Pompoco et al., 2017; Hunt and Dumville, 2016; Hall, 2015; Kurlychek et al., 2012; Kelso, 2000; Robinson, 1990; Anderson, 1981).

A few strengths can be attributed to this study. Among them are that the study systematically investigated 50 diverse and quality studies and, in the process, pool 71 combined effect size estimates from the studies in the attempt to ascertain aggregate estimates of the relationship between correctional education and offender recidivism. These are a sizable number of studies and effect size estimates that could enable deeper insights to be gained and critical lessons gleaned in the study of the relationship between participation in prison-based education and offender recidivism. Even though a plausible case can be made that the method utilized here may be lacking in some respects, it would be reasonable to submit that the study made some serious attempts to reduce the potential sources of bias in the study by employing regression coefficients method which is known to be helpful in reducing sources of potential bias in the results of studies of this kind (e.g., Scott, 2018; Drake and Fumia, 2017; Pompoco et al., 2017; Ioannidis et al., 2017; Hedges et al., 2010).

However, it can be argued that a major weakness of this study was that it did not employ a more rigorous publication bias correction methodological approach (Ioannidis et al., 2017; Stanley and Doucouliagos, 2014) as Fogarty and Giles (2018) did in their replication study and were able to find that there is strong evidence of publication bias in some of the literature examined in Davis et al. (2013) meta-analysis study. However, after employing the more rigorous methodological design that corrected the identifiable publication bias features in the Davis et al. (2013) study, Fogarty and Giles (2018) observed that there is still strong and clear evidence indicating a large and statistically significant reduction of the risk of recidivism following participation in most of the education correctional programs.

Other research that met the criteria used for the selection of empirical literature for review for this chapter was published by Hall (2015). In the efforts to systematically ascertain factors that are attributed to recidivism so that research trajectory can be focused toward the most promising recidivism reduction tool, the researcher carried out a meta-analysis of 10 empirical studies that were conducted on correctional education and recidivism from 1995 to 2010 which sought to show whether correctional education has an impact on recidivism reduction. In the study, various recidivism reduction tools were identified. Among them are offenders' age, race, gender, marital status, and educational attainment and employment. These recidivism reduction tools can also be referred to as risk factors that influence recidivism (Duwe, 2017).

Of all the various recidivism reduction tools identified in the study, correctional education programming, especially at the postsecondary levels, appears to offer the most promising recidivism reduction tool. This assertion is evident in that the study clearly shows that of all the 10 empirical studies systematically reviewed and analyzed, correctional education appears to have the greatest positive impact on offender recidivism. The finding of this study supports the results of those found in the growing body of empirical literature on the subject which show that correctional education programs in general have a positive impact on recidivism and more so when the level of education increases up to college levels (for example, Denney and Tynes, 2021; Kim and Clark, 2013; Nally et al., 2012; Steurer et al., 2010; Brazell, et al., 2009; Winterfield et al., 2009; Butiuk et al., 2005; Chappell, 2004; Erisman and

Contardo, 2005; Gordon and Weldon, 2003; Lipsey and Cullen, 2007; Steurer et al., 2001; Hull et al., 2000).

This study has a number of important strengths. Among them are that the study was well researched and presented. It identifies various factors and/or tools that potentially influence recidivism and systematically analyzes them in ways that are probing enough so that some critical lessons can be gleaned, and deeper insights gained in the process. For instance, the study systematically identifies and critically analyzes the factors that seem to interact between correctional education and offender recidivism so that future research can focus on the tools that appear to be the most promising for recidivism reduction. The study also identifies and systemically explains characteristics of some of the major potential problems in the study of these kinds of subjects, such as self-selection bias (Fogarty and Giles, 2018; Duwe, 2017; Batiuk et al., 2005) and definition/measurement of recidivism (Scott, 2018), which a lot of studies that have been conducted on the subject ignore and/or poorly analyze such that certain characteristics are left unexplored or poorly explored and as a result leave no clear picture of their influence on correctional education and offender recidivism. In addition, the study also identifies and acknowledges the inability of any of the 10 studies it reviews to control the risk factors of recidivism (age, gender, race, marital status, employment, and educational attainment). Instead, few, if any, of the risk factors were controlled in the studies it reviewed.

On the other hand, some weaknesses can be attributed to the study. One of those weaknesses is the inability of the study to acknowledge prior criminal record as a major risk factor of recidivism. Such risk factor ought to be explored along with the other risk factors of recidivism (i.e., age, gender, race, marital status, employment, and educational attainment) identified and analyzed by the study. Not doing so is problematic in that research shows that prior history of criminal behavior and educational attainment/employment status are the most important risk factors of offender recidivism (e.g., Fogarty and Giles, 2018; Scott, 2018; Duwe, 2017; Drake and Fumia, 2017; Duwe and Clark, 2014; Davis et al, 2013; Contardo and Tolbert, 2008).

Another issue that could be considered problematic with this study is the suggestion that reconviction is the most suitable measure of recidivism and as well as claims that it captures the most crime and is commonly used as the indicator of guilt in the U.S. criminal justice system. As has been demonstrated with vigor in this book in several instances, the suggestion that reconviction is the most suitable indicator of recidivism flies in the face of documented evidence in most literature on the subject as well as deep and critical reasoning (e.g., Delisi and Conis, 2019; Berghuis, 2018; Scott, 2018; Kim and Clark, 2013; Chappell, 2004: Ubah, 2002; Steven and Ward, 1997; Meiser, 1989) and is therefore questionable at best.

The truth of the matter is that most literature on the subject suggests that the use of rearrest and/or reconviction as indicators of recidivism are more problematic than the use of reinstitutionalization, especially when we are dealing with reincarceration. This is so because, with respect to incarceration, the definition of recidivism encompasses "a return to prison" which shows the full measure of guilt than reconviction in the criminal justice system process—so much so because not all parolees rearrested and/or reconvicted do return to prison. Therefore, instead of conceptualizing reconviction as the most suitable measure of recidivism as suggested by Hall (2015), reinstitutionalization into a correctional institution as a measure of recidivism has been described as a much more appropriate and acceptable indicator in most scholarly literature on the subject (e.g., Delisi and Conis, 2019; Berghuis, 2018; Scott, 2018; Kim and Clark, 2013; Chappell, 2004; Ubah, 2002; Steven and Ward, 1997; Meiser, 1989). This is so because the measure means that the ex-inmate has been rearrested, reprocessed, reconvicted, and reincarcerated into the custody of a correctional institution (state or federal), either because of a technical violation or because of committing a new offense, or both. Based on this well-established evidence, it is appropriate that future studies on the subject make use of reinstitutionalization as an indicator of recidivism instead of rearrest and/or reconviction.

Further, a comprehensive recidivism study among federal offenders conducted by the United States Sentencing Commission (2016) in which the three measures of recidivism—rearrest, reconviction, and reinstitutionalized—were utilized offers a useful insight into the efforts to ascertain the degree of their suitability and acceptability as a measure of recidivism. The findings of the study show differing recidivism rates among them (i.e., 49.3 percent were rearrested, 31.7 percent were reconvicted, and 24.6 percent were reinstitutionalized). This observed difference of lower outcome recidivism rate with the measure of reinstitutionalization has more to do with the fact that the measure has much more exhaustive steps in the criminal justice system process than the other two measures. This is so because for an offender to be reinstitutionalized back to a correctional center, that offender must first be rearrested and reconvicted. And this is one of the major attributes and strengths of reinstitutionalization that makes it have a greater appeal and acceptability as the most effective, reliable, and credible indicator of recidivism than does rearrest and reconviction (e.g., Delisi and Conis, 2019; Berghuis, 2018; Scott, 2018; Kim and Clark, 2013; Chappell, 2004; Ubah, 2002; Steven and Ward, 1997; Meiser, 1989).

Using a highly regarded publication bias corrections method (Ioannidis et al., 2017; Stanley and Doucouliagos, 2014) as a yardstick, Fogarty and Giles (2018) replicated Davis et al. (2013) meta-analysis of 50 studies that investigated the effects of correctional education programs on recidivism without utilizing the publication bias correction method. Apart from this feature, Fogarty and Giles made use of just about all the other methods that were utilized in the Davis et al. (2013) study, such as reincarceration as a model outcome measure of recidivism as well as one and three years after release from prison as a follow-up at-risk period of recidivism as a model measurement period.

Fogarty and Giles (2018) find that there is strong evidence of publication bias in some of the empirical literature examined in the Davis et al. (2013) meta-analysis study. After correcting for those identifiable publication bias features, Fogarty and Giles (2018) observed that there is still strong and clear evidence indicating a large and statistically significant reduction of the risk of recidivism following participation in both the basic education correctional programs and postsecondary correctional programs. This result is in line with those found in a growing body of recent studies on the subject that indicate that participation in a prison-based education program, especially at the postsecondary levels, has a clear reduction on recidivism rates (e.g., Pelletier and Evans, 2019; Evans, 2018; Fogarty and Giles, 2018: Duwe, 2017; Pompoco et al., 2017; Karpowitz, 2017; Hall, 2015; Ginsberg, 2014; Lewen, 2014; Davis et al., 2013; Kim and Clark, 2013; Steurer et al, 2010; Brazell et al, 2009). However, the result of reduction of the risk of recidivism following participation in vocation education programs was less clear. According to the researchers, this result of vocational programs suggests that there are many low power studies in the programs which make the tendency for statistically significant result to be an outlier observation as well as the vocational education programs estimate to be relatively imprecise.

Several strengths can be attributed to this study. Perhaps the most prominent among them is that the study employed a more rigorous methodological approach than that utilized in Davis et al. (2013) as well as in many other previous studies that have been conducted on the subject. Using a well-established publication bias correction method (Ioannidis et al., 2017; Stanley and Doucouliagos, 2014) as a distinctive yardstick, Fogarty and Giles enables us to gain deeper insights and understanding of some of the interacting social processes at work in the relationship between prison-based education programs and offender recidivism an in the process, learned some critical lessons. These are lessons that might be too important and too costly to ignore in 21st century correctional research, practice, and policy.

In the same vein, Denney and Tynes (2021) conducted an impact assessment study that examined the effects of participation in the college-in-prison program of the Bard Prison Initiative (BPI) in New York. To be clear, BPI is a liberal arts college that has offered postsecondary education for incarcerated men and women since 2001. Just as at its main campus in Annandale, Bard College offers both the Associate of Arts (A.A.) program and the Bachelor of

Arts (B.A.) program at six correctional institutions across New York State. Five out of the six facilities are for men while the other facility is for women. Three of these prisons are classified as maximum security institutions and the other three are medium security. Participating students in the BPI need a total of 60 credits hours to be awarded the A.A. degree and 120 credits hours to earn a B.A. degree.

Students are admitted to the Bard college-in-prison program through a multi-stage admission process that was designed to significantly mitigate selection and self-selection bias with the study population. The design included an in-depth knowledge of BPI admission process, testable assumptions, and key covariates. Denney and Tynes limited their study sample to those who applied to participate in the BPI college program with the intent of accounting for self-selection bias. They also utilized multi-stage admission process to help mitigate potential self-selection bias. And they did so by using the different stages to test whether selection bias was operative in the admission process. The study compared the recidivism rates of BPI participants to a similar group of those who apply, interview, but were not selected to participate. The total number of the study population who were selected for interview (i.e., the last stage in the BPI admission process) was 683. Of this number, 324 were admitted into the BPI program whereas 359 were rejected.

Findings of the study reveal that there was a large and significant reduction in recidivism rates among those inmates who participated in the BPI than inmates who did not. This finding is consistent with those found in a growing body of empirical literature on the subject, especially the most recent ones which overwhelmingly indicate that participation in a prison-based education program, especially at the postsecondary levels, has enough clear evidence of reduction on recidivism rates (e.g., Pelletier and Evans, 2019; Evans, 2018; Fogarty and Giles, 2018: Duwe, 2017; Pompoco et al., 2017; Karpowitz, 2017; Hall, 2015; Ginsberg, 2014; Lewen, 2014; Davis et al., 2013; Kim and Clark, 2013; Steurer et al., 2010; Brazell et al., 2009). The researchers also found that reduction on recidivism was consistent with racial groupings and that the people who participated in the program at a higher level recidivated at much lower rates than those who did not. These findings are consistent with those find in a growing body of research on the subject.

Several strengths can be attributed to this study. Perhaps the most striking one has to do with the kind of method utilized in the study. This is so because there appears to be a significant improvement in the efforts to account for the effect of selection and self-selection bias in the study, thereby substantially reducing their potential bias effects. The merit of this strength can be found in the design-based approach utilized in the study which involved the use of a multi-stage admission process in admitting inmates to the college thereby significantly reducing identifiable differences that might have existed between the two groups studied. The multi-stage admission process signifies acknowledgment of the problems of "selection and self-selection" in the study of these kinds of subjects and takes serious steps to significantly mitigate the potential problem. The issue of selection and self-selection bias is a very serious problem with the reliability of the results of these kinds of studies because it raises the legitimate question of whether lowered propensity to recidivate is an effect of exposure to educational programs or whether the propensity to rehabilitate causes both participation in educational programs and successful parole. Put differently, these potential problems, as such, are very serious issues because they raise the question of whether actual participation in the program or the motivation to participate in the program is responsible for the impact on recidivism (see, for example, Scott, 2018; Kim and Clark, 2013; Anderson, 1981).

Generally, one is tempted to agree that the motivation to participate in the program is much more responsible for the impact on recidivism than actual participation in the program. This is so because parolees' participation in a postsecondary correctional program does not result in greater readiness not to recidivate to the life of crime. Instead, the increased readiness not to recidivate to the life of crime and the interest in participating in prison education programs are the result of the parolees' decision to do what it takes to bring their lives into order. Thus, some general restructuring of outlook, perhaps a sort of conversion, may be the main factor in determining whether a previously incarcerated and released offender will recidivate; whether that offender participated in the prison-based postsecondary education or not appears to be more of an indicator of the presence of such a new outlook than its cause. If an offender participated in a correctional education program but has not really decided to "go straight" when released into the larger society, that offender would be most likely to go back to the life of crime. On the other hand, if an offender did not participate in postsecondary correctional education programming because of lack of opportunity but had already decided to "go straight," it is more likely that when that offender is released into the larger community he or she would not engage in antisocial behavior.

After all, lack of participation in prison-based college education can mean several things, such as either the lack of opportunity to get into the program or the lack of willingness to go straight, or both. It is important to keep in mind that lack of opportunity to participate in postsecondary correctional education does not go together with the lack of willingness to go straight. It simply means that the inmate could not participate in the program due to lack of chance to do so, which does mean the lack of determination to change from criminality. In such a case, inmate participation or lack of participation in a postsecondary correctional program is not and cannot be the main determining factor of whether that inmate will recidivate or not when released into the larger community. Instead, having embraced a new attitude toward life is the main determining factor. This is so because even if an inmate had the opportunity to participate in the program but did not want to change from his criminal ways of life, participation by itself would not make any difference in how that inmate would perform when released into the larger society.

On the other hand, some weaknesses can be attributed to this study. They include lack of clear acknowledgment of prior criminal record of the subjects studied, which is a major risk factor of recidivism study; incomplete parole records; and the reluctance of ex-offenders to cooperate in the interview. To be clear, the inability of the study to acknowledge prior criminal record as a major risk factor of recidivism study is a serious issue. This is so because such risk factor ought to be explored along with the other risk factors of recidivism (age, gender, race, marital status, employment, and educational attainment) identified and analyzed by the study. Not doing so is problematic, in that research shows that prior history of criminal behavior and educational attainment/employment status are the most important risk factors of offender recidivism (e.g., Fogarty and Giles, 2018; Scott, 2018; Duwe, 2017; Drake and Fumia, 2017; Duwe and Clark, 2014; Davis et al., 2013; Contardo and Tolbert, 2008).

Lessons Learned from the Studies of 2011–2022

Several lessons can be gleaned from the studies of 2011–2022 examined above. Most prominent among them is that the studies of 2011–2022 can be said to represent a more methodologically rigorous research design that addresses some of the inherent problems in the study of these kinds of subjects. For example, a number of studies of 2011–2022 not only recognized the issue of self-selection bias in these kinds of studies but also took reasonable steps to address the problem adequately such as by utilizing more methodically rigorous methods that address and minimize the issue in a manner that is sound enough (Davis et al., 2013; Drake and Fumia, 2017; Fogarty and Giles, 2018; Hall, 2015; Ioannidis et al., 2017; Kim and Clark, 2013; Nally et al., 2012; Pompoco et al., 2017; Stanley and Doucouliagos, 2014); also the results of the studies of 2011–2022 show a much more robust positive effect on the recidivism rates of prisoners who participated in prison-based postsecondary education programs than those who did not.

SUMMARIZING THE GENERAL LESSONS LEARNED FROM THE PRISON-BASED REHABILITATION EMPIRICAL STUDIES OF 1945–2022

As Gerber and Fritsch (1995) instruct, it is better for scholars to be guided by a small number of quality studies characterized by their insightfulness and strengths than by a large quantity of studies that are too weak, lack imagination, and fail to be probing. In the selection of literature for review in this chapter, serious efforts were made to heed this advice and, as a result, eliminated a good deal of literature not specifically focused on prison-based rehabilitative education programs and/or seriously lacking in insightfulness and strengths.

However, the empirical studies reviewed here have enabled us to learn a great deal about the debate over prison-based education. Using Martinson's (1974) controversial study as a reference point was insightful because it systematically enables us to examine the empirical studies that dealt with the subject matter through the following seven useful processes: pre-Martinson's evaluative studies; studies published within Martinson's investigative periods 1945–1967; a study published the year Martinson's "nothing works" report came out; evaluative studies of the late 1970s through 1980s; prison-based impact assessments of the 1990s; a review of correctional education treatment studies of 2000–2010; and a review of prison-based rehabilitation impact assessment studies of 2011–2022.

Martinson's "nothing works" verdict on correctional education is the most cited criminological literature on the subject and the most controversial. But the question of whether Martinson was right or wrong in his conclusion that nothing works, is not clearly established by literature examined across all different investigative periods utilized in this chapter. What appears to be the case was that the literature examined and analyzed in more recent investigative periods tends to show more positive outcomes with prison-based rehabilitation programs than earlier ones. However, taken together, it is this author's conclusion that the findings of empirical studies found in the course of this study lend support to the idea that participation in a prison-based postsecondary education program apparently serves to differentiate the more successful parolees from the unsuccessful ones (e.g., Fogarty and Giles, 2018; Drake and Fumia, 2017; Pompoco et al., 2017; Hall, 2015; Stanley and Doucouliagos, 2014; Kim and Clark, 2013; Nally et al., 2012; Lipsey and Cullen, 2007; Ubah, 2002; Jenkins et al., 1995; Robinson, 1990; Holloway and Moke, 1986; Anderson, 1981; Matisoff, 1973; Zink, 1962; Fox, 1950; Schnur, 1948).

Perhaps the most important lesson learned from the review was that, unlike more recent investigative period studies, most of the early investigative period studies examined essentially limited themselves to the establishment of a statistical association between inmate participation in correctional education and offender recidivism. However, they said little regarding the causal patterns underlying this association. They seemed to share an assumption of the causal effectiveness of exposure to educational programs as a sort of protection against recidivism, but they left unspecified just what it is about correctional education programs that leads to the attenuation of offender recidivism. Simply put, these studies stopped precisely at a point where more analysis was required. The very few that mentioned causality did not deal with it adequately in the sense that the theoretical ramifications of such spuriousness were left unexplored. In fact, the problem of "self-selection bias," i.e., of the overrepresentation, among education participants, of inmates already predisposed not to recidivate is a very serious issue. Yet it was slighted by most of the earlier time periods studies reviewed here. An examination and analysis of the issue in the studies of more recent time periods tends to fill the void, at least to a certain extent. Yet a lot more work needs to be done on the issue. Therefore, in this book, this author is calling on future studies on the subjects to make more serious efforts to systematically explore the issue more vigorously and critically. In doing so, they should try to go beyond statistical association analysis by raising the issue of spurious relationship ignored by a lot of studies conducted in the earlier time periods and then make adequate efforts to explore the theoretical ramifications of the issue.

We also learned about the failure of some of the studies reviewed here to clearly specify the program category or categories that made up the criterion group and the control group. They caused this problem by referring to the criterion group as program participants. Without much explicit justification, they treated program completers and noncompleters as a homogenous group of program participants. By the same token, they made a similar decision by referring to the comparison group as nonprogram graduates without distinguishing between program noncompleters and those who did not participate at all in the programs. These categories are distinctive program groups that should not be considered similar without good reasons.

Another shortcoming of much of the reviewed literature is the absence of good descriptive information concerning the educational programs in prison. It is conceivable that, regarding the reduction of recidivism, some types of prison-based education programs are more effective than others. As a result, education should not be viewed as some uniform and homogeneous entity, exposure to which alters thinking and motivation invariably in the same fashion (Ubah, 2014, 2000).

There is an important issue in corrections education operations that most of the above reviewed studies failed to consider, namely, that of the adequacy of the educational offerings to the effective demand for them. The issue came to the fore more so with the onset of major external changes (the end of federal Pell Grants for correctional education programming in 1994) which seemed to profoundly negatively affect correctional education programming and perhaps offender recidivism across the nation. This is evident as research shows that the elimination of the Pell Grants led to cutbacks in the funding for most of the correctional rehabilitative programs in the United States. As a result, most of prison-based postsecondary education programs in most states were completely phased out of existence due to lack of funds (Latessa at el., 2015; Ubah, 2001; Petersilia, 2000; Tewksbury and Taylor, 1996). According to the Center on Crime, Community and Culture (1997), the elimination of Pell monies for correctional education has forced more than one-half of correctional institutions in each state to make cuts over the five years preceding its report in their inmate education budgets, with some jurisdictions eliminating such programs entirely. There is widespread agreement by wardens and directors of correctional education programs across the nation of the adverse impact of the end of inmate education Pell Grants in 1994 (Tewksbury and Taylor, 1996:62). However, only a few studies mentioned the emergence of the Second Chance Act and the Second Chance Pell Pilot Initiative which partially ended the ban on prisons-based Pell Grants and once again began to give prisoners at select sites access to federal monies for postsecondary education especially from 2016. This is easily understandable because these latest developments in the funding of college in prison programs are a relatively recent occurrence.

In conclusion, it may be said, then, that a lot of the studies reviewed above are suggestive but not conclusive on the point that participation in and/or completion of correctional education programs significantly reduces offender recidivism. Early studies on the issue seemed not to show as much of a significant relationship between exposure to correctional education and lower rates of recidivism as do recent ones. The literature findings seem to suggest at least three things:

1. That our correctional education programs are now more rehabilitative than earlier ones;
2. That our earlier researchers did not conduct their studies as well as later ones; or
3. That there have been changes in the inmate population's attitudes.

This author thinks it is a little bit of all three.

Chapter 5

Reaffirming the Limits of Offender Rehabilitation but with Caution

Offender rehabilitation is one of the major goals of the correctional system. However, the debate over offender rehabilitation continues to divide scholars (Ubah, 2014; Taylor and Tewksbury, 2002). Some scholars argue that it does not work (e.g., Sullivan, 1990; Goredki, 1979; Martinson, 1974), while others think that it does work (e.g., Denney and Tynes, 2021; Vandala, 2019; Jenkins et al., 1995; Porporino and Robinson, 1992; Schumacker et al., 1990). And since prison-based education, especially at the postsecondary level, is a significant offender rehabilitation program, it is made the focus of this analysis. Recidivism rate is mostly used to determine the usefulness or lack of prison-based offender rehabilitation programs. However, using recidivism rate as a sole assessment of prison-based education programs cast undue doubt on the usefulness of the programs. This chapter, therefore, reaffirms the limits of offender rehabilitation, but with caution that it may be too important and too costly for criminology, criminal justice, public policy, and the public at large to ignore in any assessment of the usefulness of offender rehabilitation programs.

THE REHABILITATIVE IDEAL

Correctional education programs, especially at the postsecondary level, are designed on the notion that a degree of offender rehabilitation can be achieved through them, i.e., that offenders' exposure to such programs is a contributory cause to lowered recidivism. The theories that suggest this notion include, but are not limited to, moral development theory, social psychological development theory, and opportunity theory (e.g., Ubah and

Ubah, 2019; Ubah and Robinson, 2002; Taylor and Tewksbury, 2002). These theories are also described as "optimistic perspective," and central to them, as they are articulated by penologists, criminologists, sociologists, educators, and public figures, is the assumption that correctional educational programs can enhance the successful reintegration of certain individual inmates from the society of captives into the general society (e.g., Vandala, 2019; Johnson, 2002; Clemmer, 1958; Sykes, 1958). These optimistic theories can also be referred to as "theories of individual change." Theories of individual change focus directly on the individual as the point of analysis, and only indirectly on the larger society. In other words, responsibility for recidivism reduction, as an outcome of inmate education, depends to the individual inmates.

The question then is, what is it about correctional treatment programs that reduces offender recidivism: its building of moral character, self-esteem, and self-concept; its provision of a new perspective on life with attendant reorientation of action; its function as a coping mechanism; the know-how it provides; new interests; its function as a credential in the labor market. The theoretical approaches that address some of these questions have been discussed (e.g., Ubah and Ubah, 2019; Ubah and Robinson, 2002).

In sum, idealistic theories suggest that the idea of prison-based college education aspect of offender rehabilitation indicates the right step in the right direction, because the programs can promote change in some inmates, improve their psychological well-being, and offer them credentials for the labor market. The premises of the idealistic theories form the arsenal from which proponents of correctional education programs draw their arguments for the continued provision and improvement of prison-based college education.

Although these idealistic perspectives articulate interesting views of crime causation, some issues remain unaddressed within these perspectives. Central among these issues is the problem of "self-selection" (i.e., offenders who are predisposed to rehabilitate). Also, regarding postsecondary correctional education programs, generally one may wonder how education, which so often seems ineffective in the larger society, has the capacity to accomplish so much under the harsh conditions of prison life.

The Limits of Rehabilitative Ideal

Several limitations exist with the rehabilitative ideal. For example, Anderson (1981), in his analysis of parole success, made a very important point that "it could be that many parolees who are motivated to become involved in vocational training are similarly motivated to be good employees, regardless of the initial placement." Anderson here presents a picture that differs from that drawn by many advocates of rehabilitative programs who assume that lowered propensity to recidivate in the life of crime is an effect of exposure to correctional program. Anderson, in contrast, suggests that the propensity to rehabilitate causes both participation in correctional education programs and successful rehabilitation and reintegration.

The strength of Anderson's study rests on the number of parole success criteria utilized, qualitative knowledge of the programs studied, as well as the random selection technique employed in the selection of 50 employers of vocationally trained parolees, and perhaps more importantly, the acknowledgment of the problems of "self-selection" in the study of these subjects.

Because of the importance of the issue here, it cannot be overemphasized that the issue of self-selection is very serious because it raises the question of whether actual participation in the program or the motivation to participate in the program is more responsible for the impact on recidivism. This author believes that the motivation to participate in the program is much more responsible for the impact on recidivism than the actual participation in the program. This is because offenders' participation in a correctional program does not result in greater readiness not to recidivate to the life of crime. Instead, the increased readiness not to recidivate and the interest in participating in correctional programs are the result of the offenders' decision to do what it takes to bring their lives into order.

Thus, some general restructuring of outlook, perhaps a sort of conversion, may be the main factor in determining whether a previously convicted and released offender will recidivate; whether that offender participated in a correctional treatment program or not appears to be more of an indicator of the presence of such a new outlook than its cause. If an offender participated in a correctional rehabilitation program but has not really decided to "go straight" when released into the larger society, that offender would be most likely to go back to the life of crime. On the other hand, if an offender did not participate in correctional programming because of lack of opportunity but had already decided to "go straight" anyway, it is more likely that when that offender is released into the larger community he or she would not engage in antisocial behavior.

After all, lack of participation in a correctional program can mean several things, such as the lack of opportunity to get into the program or the lack of willingness to go straight, or both. It is important to keep in mind that lack of opportunity to participate in a correctional rehabilitative program does not go together with the lack of willingness to go straight. It simply means that the offender could not participate in a correctional program due to lack of chance, which does not mean the lack of determination to change from criminality.

In such a case, offender participation or lack of participation in a correctional rehabilitation program is not and cannot be the main determining factor of whether that offender will recidivate to the life of crime or not. Instead, having embraced a new attitude toward life is the main determining factor. This is so because even if an offender had the opportunity to participate in correctional programming but did not want to change from his criminal ways of life, participation by itself would not make any difference to how that offender would perform in the future (Knepper, 2003; Ubah, 2002). All said and done, this is not to suggest that "nothing works" with correctional education programs. In fact, they do work some of the time for certain offenders (e.g., Denney and Tynes, 2021; Vandala, 2019; Jenkins et al., 1995; Porporino and Robinson, 1992; Anderson, 1991). Nevertheless, what about other considerations of correctional education programs?

But with Caution

It is imperative that criminology, criminal justice, public policy personnel, and the public in general take adequate caution in any assessment of the usefulness or lack of it of prison-based education programs as determined by recidivism rate reduction. This is because prison-based education programs especially at the postsecondary level were not only meant to provide inmates with skills and credentials for recidivism rate reduction as they attempted to make a transition from the society of captives into the general society (Sykes, 1958), but also have other important values such as academic, employment signaling, institutional function, and social considerations (e.g., Denney and Tynes, 2021; Pompoco et al., 2017; Clear, 2011; Maruna, 2012; Ubah, 2014; Gaes, 2008).

An examination of these other values of the programs is scholarly significant, in that, among other things, it would go beyond the status quo upon which the subject has been examined previously. It would enable us to have broader and deeper insights and understanding of the academic debate over prison-based education and the offender recidivism rate. It would provide broader and deeper understanding and lessons that may be too important and too costly to ignore in 21st century criminology, criminal justice, and public policy. It would help policy makers have broader and deeper insights and understanding of the interacting processes and factors at work as they make critical decisions about whether the program should continue to exist, and if so, how it should be structured, administered, and funded. It would help send signals to employers as they make employment decisions on whether to hire an ex-offender or not. And it would shed deeper and broader insights on some of the social issues and factors concerning prison-based education programs and offender recidivism rates. As a result, the chapter that follows provides a more detailed discussion of these important values and/or considerations of prison-based postsecondary education programs.

SUMMARY

This chapter reaffirms the limits of offender rehabilitation but with cautions that can be too important and too costly for criminology, criminal justice, public policy, and the public at large to ignore in any assessment of the usefulness or lack of it of prison-based education programs. The chapter argues that the rehabilitative ideals are speculative and not specific enough regarding the relationship between prison-based postsecondary education programming and offender recidivism. Nonetheless, they articulate interesting ideas regarding rehabilitative programs and offender recidivism. It suggests that the association between correctional education attainment while in prison and the lives of formally incarcerated persons when they return to the larger community is not satisfactorily captured by one simple measure of success or failure because there is a whole web of other interacting processes and factors that make reintegration from prison into the general society difficult. For this reason, a consideration of multiple criteria and not just recidivism rates will be the right step in the right direction.

To reiterate, it stresses very strongly that any assessment of the usefulness or lack of it of prison-based education programs and offender recidivism must account for its other relevant considerations, which include but are not limited to academic, employment signaling, institutional function, policy, and social considerations. These other considerations are discussed in more detail in the next chapter. Finally, when all is said and done, the debate over prison-based education programs has not been resolved. Instead, it continues to divide scholars, policy makers, correctional practitioners, and the public in general. As such, more studies are needed for better understanding and deeper insights on the subject.

Chapter 6

Using Recidivism Rate as the Sole Indicator of Prison-Based Rehabilitation Usefulness

Several scholars hold the view that a degree of inmate rehabilitation and reintegration can be achieved through prison-based education programs, that is, that inmates' exposure to such education programs is a contributing cause of lowered recidivism and productive citizenship. These perspectives can be sociological, biological, psychological, and economically deterministic in nature (e.g., Williams and McShane, 2014; Paparozzi and Guy, 2014; Lilly et al., 2010; Ward and Maruna, 2007). However, the perspectives collectively can be referred to as idealistic/optimistic rehabilitation perspectives. Idealistic and/or optimistic rehabilitation perspectives include but are not limited to moral-development perspective, social-psychological development perspective, and opportunity perspective (Ubah and Ubah, 2019; Ubah and Robinson, 2002).

Central to these idealistic/optimistic perspectives, as articulated by penologists, criminologists, sociologists, educators, and public figures, is an assumption that correctional education programs can enhance the successful reintegration of some individual inmates from the society of captives into the general society (e.g., Vandala, 2019; Evans, 2018; Bushway and Apel, 2012; Hipp et al., 2010; Bui and Morash, 2010; Wang et al., 2010; Ward and Maruna, 2007; Cullen, 2007; Travis, 2009; Ubah and Robinson, 2002; Stevens and Ward, 1997; Sykes, 1958). In other words, these perspectives can be referred to collectively, as "perspectives of individual change" (e.g., Ubah and Ubah, 2019; Ubah and Robinson, 2002). Perspectives of individual change focus directly on the individual offender as the point of analysis and only indirectly on the larger society. For a detailed accounting of the foundations of rehabilitation theories, see, for example, Ward and Maruna, 2007.

Nonetheless, the question, then, is what is it about a prison-based education program that reduces offender recidivism? Is it its building of moral character, self-esteem, and concept of the self? Is it its provision of a new perspective on life, with attendant reorientation of action? Its function as a coping mechanism? The know-how it provides? New interests? Its function as a credential in the labor market? The theoretical approaches and empirical evidence that address some of these questions have been discussed by Ubah and Ubah, 2019; Bushway and Apel, 2012; Cullen and Gilbert, 2013; Latessa, 2012; Hipp et al., 2010; Ubah and Robinson, 2002; Ward and Maruna, 2007, among others.

As the all-time great Greek classical philosopher Socrates asserts, "Unexamined life is not worth living" (Basic, 2021; Jablecki, 2000). The author thinks that this well-established wisdom should also be heeded in the analysis of the issue of prison-based offender rehabilitation programs. Unfortunately, most studies of correctional education have focused on the debate over whether prison-based education programs work or do not work as determined only by recidivism rate (e.g., Anderson, 1981; Cullen et al., 2011; Jenkins et al., 1995; Lattimore et al., 2010; Petersilia, 2004; Porporino and Robinson, 1992; Martinson, 1974), while, to a great degree, they have ignored the need to account for other important considerations. This chapter, therefore, argues that in addition to offender recidivism rate, adequate attention should be given to other important considerations like academic, employment signaling, institutional function, and social values of prison-based education programs in any determination of the usefulness or lack of it of the programs.

This paradigm shifts from the way the usefulness or lack of it of prison-based education programs is mostly determined previously is academically significant, in that, among other things, it would enable us to have broader and deeper insights and understanding of the academic debate over prison-based education programs and offender recidivism. It would provide broader and deeper insights and lessons that may be too important and too costly to ignore in 21st century criminology, criminal justice, and public policy. It would help policy makers to have broader and deeper insights and understanding of the interacting processes at work as they make critical decisions about whether the programs should continue to exist, and if so, how they should be structured, administered, and funded. It would help send useful signals to employers as they make employment decisions on whether or not to hire an ex-offender. And it would shed deeper and broader light on some of the social issues concerning prison-based education programs and offender recidivism rates. The following are discussions of those other important considerations' value of the subject.

CONSIDERATIONS OF PRISON-BASED EDUCATION PROGRAM USEFULNESS

There are several important values that can be considered in any determination of the usefulness of prison-based education programs. Those values include but may be limited to recidivism rate considerations value, employment signaling considerations value, social considerations value, and institutional considerations value. What follows are some discussions of them, beginning with recidivism rate considerations value.

Recidivism Rate Considerations Value

Offender recidivism rate is the dominant measure of rehabilitative correctional programs' success or failure and for some important reasons (e.g., Crow and Smykla, 2014; Ward and Maruna, 2007; Ogloff and Davis, 2004; Ubah, 2001; Martinson, 1974). As a result, any assessment of the usefulness or lack of it of prison-based education programs must account for its recidivism rate. But the question remains. What is important about recidivism rate considerations value of prison-based education programs?

Recidivism rate considerations value of prison-based education programs among parolees whom it serves is imperative for effective correctional planning and programming. As such, any assessment of the usefulness of prison-based education programs must account for their recidivism rate considerations value (e.g., Petersilia, 2004; Robinson, 1990; Mandel, 1963). For instance, Mandel (1963:2) states that:

> Without the studies on recidivism, it is impossible to compare the efficacy of correctional programs among correctional agencies and institutions. With the studies it becomes feasible to focus attention upon those programs which appear to have the greatest salutary effects upon the offenders whom they reach.

In line with Mandel's insightful suggestions, Robinson (1990) articulates what I think encompasses a great deal of the potential policy implications of recidivism rate considerations value of studies of prison-based education programs. He stresses that studies on offender recidivism rates will aid policy makers and correctional administrators in making critical decisions about whether rehabilitative programs should exist and, if so, how they should be structured, administered, and funded; they will aid policy makers and correctional administrators in identifying effective and viable rehabilitative programs; and they will enable them to focus attention upon the programs which appear to have the greatest efficacy upon the offenders they serve. Studies of these programs may also assist correctional administrators in identifying variables that serve as predictors of inmate success in the programs and predictors of successful program utilization.

As imperative as recidivism rate considerations value is with prison-based education programs, it is important to note that any assessment of the usefulness or lack of it of prison-based education programs as measured by offender recidivism rate should also account for its other important considerations, such as academic, employment signaling, institutional function, and social considerations value of the programs. The questions, then, are:

1. What is it about academic considerations value of prison-based education programs?
2. What is it about employment signaling considerations value of prison-based education programs?
3. What is it about institutional function considerations value of prison-based education programs?
4. What is it about social considerations value of prison-based education programs?
5. What are the lessons learned from the examination of the values of these considerations, and the importance of such lessons for 21st century criminology, criminal justice, public policy, and the public in general?

The following are attempts to address the questions.

Academic Considerations Value

The debate over prison-based education, which continues to divide scholars, adds to the academic discussion considerations value of the programs. Some argue that, to a considerable extent, such education programs accomplish their purpose, namely, significant rate of recidivism reduction (e.g., Denney and Tynes, 2021; Vandala; 2019; Duwe, 2018; Anderson, 1981; Jenkins et al., 1995; Porporino and Robinson, 1992; Schumacker et al., 1990), whereas others think that it does not work (e.g., Wilkinson and Pickett, 2010; Martinson, 1974; Sullivan, 1990). Central to the debate are two contradictory perspectives on prison-based education programs: (a) an idealistic/optimistic view stressing its promise and value; and (b) a pessimistic reaction to its perceived ineffectiveness (Ubah and Robinson, 2002). A critical and rigorous ongoing debate over the usefulness of the programs provides enriched academic values because such undertaking adds to and enables a deeper and broader understanding and insights of the interaction or lack of it of the programs and offender recidivism rates as well as greatly inform systematic observation and research. As a result, this author has rigorously and critically examined the usefulness or lack of it of prison-based education programs from the perspective of academic considerations value as well as its other important considerations beyond merely its significant rate of recidivism reduction measure.

The literature on whether prison-based education programs work or do not work as measured by significant recidivism rate reduction is not conclusive. Recent studies tend to show more success than earlier ones (e.g., Denney and Tynes, 2021; Duwe, 2018; Kurlychek et al., 2012; Grella and Rodriguez, 2011; Ward and Maruna, 2007; Tony and Farrington, 2006; Petersilia, 2004; Ogloff and Davis, 2004; Wade and de Jong, 2000). But it is not clear and sometimes very difficult to establish the interacting factors at work that may have influenced these results. However, a scrutiny of statistical association of empirical aspects of literature on prison-based education and offender recidivism has strongly suggested that it could be a spurious relationship at work (Delisi and Conis, 2019). A relationship between two variables is said to be spurious when both variables are dependent on a third variable (Meier and Toole, 2012; McKean and Byers, 2000).

The questions, then, are: (a) Should the conclusions, as they are represented in the literature of criminology, criminal justice, and public policy, end the debate over prison education and offender recidivism; and (b) Do they suggest that correctional education programs in all institutions across jurisdictions and states do not work and, as such, no further research should be conducted on the subject? The answers to both questions are clearly in the negative. It is the view of this author that the conclusions have shed some light on the ongoing debate, yet there is a need for more studies to be conducted on the subject within and across U.S. institutions and jurisdictions (Vandala, 2019).

In contrast to most investigations on the subject that used only recidivism rates as a criterion in determining the usefulness or lack of it of prison-based education programming, it is important that future studies utilize multiple criteria in assessing the usefulness or lack of it of the programs (Anderson, 1981; Petersilia, 2004; Ubah, 2014). This paradigm shift would enable us to have a broader and in-depth insight and understanding of the usefulness or lack of it of the programs. As a result, the author of this book calls on future studies on the subject to utilize multiple criteria in any determination of the usefulness or lack of it of the programs and not just with recidivism rate measurement, as is presently the case with most studies on the subject. On that note, we now turn to what is it about employment signaling considerations value of the prison-based education program?

Employment Signaling Considerations Value

Another important idea that perhaps should be considered in the discussion of the usefulness or lack of it of prison-based education programs, especially at the college level, beyond their effects on offender recidivism rate reduction is the employment signaling considerations value of the programs. Perhaps this idea in part or in whole can be captured under the framework of opportunity perspective of prison-based postsecondary education programs (Cloward and Ohlin, 1960; Edwards, 2014; Palmer, 2012). Opportunity perspective suggests that most crimes, especially crimes on the street—which are usually carried out by poor, undereducated, and disenfranchised members of a society—can be explained by a lack of viable, legitimate means to the attainment of economic opportunities (i.e., external conditions) (e.g., Bui and Morash, 2010; Herrschaft et al., 2009; Hipp et al., 2010; Ward and Maruna, 2007; Clear, 2007). This notion perhaps originated with Merton's (1938) strain theory. The strain theory suggests that deprivation, either absolute or relative, heightens feelings of anger, frustration, and confusion, which tends to result in crime (Messner and Rosenfeld, 2013; Agnew, 2001; Bernard, 1990).

Opportunity perspective, therefore, suggests that acquiring college-education credentials in prison will provide inmates with legitimate human capital (resources that influence future activities in people, such as marketable legitimate skills, trades, network relationships) that can give desistance green signals to potential employers and can open up better job opportunities and legitimate and strong social network relationships, which, in turn, can build social bonds that protect against criminal behavior (e.g., Bushway and Apel, 2012; Hershberger, 1987; Hipp et al., 2010; Hirschi, 1969; Kubrin and Stewart, 2006).

It has been well documented that going to college enables one to obtain credentials for the labor market that could open considerable opportunities and social network relationships for social mobility (e.g., Bui and Morash, 2010; Wang et al., 2010; Ellis and Lane, 1963). Thus, "the higher the attainment of education, the greater one's earning power and the greater the possibility of improving one's station in life" (Johnson, 1964:610). On the basis of this well-established finding, opportunity perspective suggests that inmates' completion of or participation in a college-level, prison-based education program is a likely desistance signal and evidence of pro-social and being engaged in the process of upward mobility, which in turn provide inmates with some necessary legitimate human-and-social capital resources (e.g., skills, knowledge, and network relationships) that can help some of them to "go straight" and abandon criminal behavior when released into the larger society (Messner and Rosenfeld, 2013; Bushway and Apel, 2012; Kurlychek et al., 2012; Latessa, 2012; Bui and Morash, 2010; Hipp et al., 2010; Kubrin and Stewart, 2006).

Thus, Hershberger (1987) notes that education in prison is a vital link, a bridge for motivated inmates who are determined to move successfully from incarceration to the real world. With their new-found academic or vocational achievements, inmates would have the rudiments of new job skills that they can polish with further education or on-the-job training. With their success in an academic or vocational classroom, they develop social skills that are necessary for the workplace. Like education in the larger society, this idea of education in prison has some currency in the public arena, not only at the national level but also at the global level as mandated in the United Nations Declarations, Standards and Conventions as human rights for all people (Universal Declaration of Human Rights, 1948; UN Standard Minimum Rules for Treatment of Prisoners, 1955); thus, former President Clinton states, "Education is the fault line, the great Continental Divide between those who will prosper and those who will not in the new economy" (Nicholas, 1996:14).

Hershberger also states that inmates' educational successes in prison seem to have generalizing effects because they tend to serve as catalysts or "hooks" that compel ex-offenders to further their education and hence improve themselves outside of prison. Through correctional education, inmates would find the motivation to go on in their educational experience, and they may be able to improve their chances of staying out of prison after completing some courses (also see, for example, Vandala, 2019).

Perhaps, this assumption about the power of prison-based education in the liberating and transformative efforts of inmates is shared so greatly by no other group than the "Convict Criminology" movement. To be clear, "Convict Criminology primarily takes the shape of essays and empirical research by convicts or ex-convicts, in possession of a Ph.D. or on their way to completing one, or enlightened academics who make critiques of existing literature, policies, and practices, and contribute a new perspective on criminology, criminal justice, corrections, and community corrections" (Richards and Ross, 2001:180).

The above assumptions of employment signaling considerations value of prison-based education programs, which were greatly captured by opportunity perspective, are in line with a major feature of the Good Live Model (GLM) of offender rehabilitation (Ward and Maruna, 2007) especially in the way the model analyzes the notion of criminogenic needs in terms of internal and external conditions. Thus, Ward and Maruna (2007:160) put it nicely:

> In order to achieve primary goods effectively in particular circumstances, it is necessary to meet two sets of conditions. First, individuals require the

> capabilities or skills required to perform good-directed actions and, by doing so, engage in the valued activity or else reach it via a series of secondary steps. Second, in order to meet human needs, it is necessary to have access to relevant opportunities, and to be supported—or, at the very least, not thwarted—by others in the process. Deficits in either of these two sets of factors would therefore make it unlikely that a person would be able to achieve what he or her set out to. He or she would be unable to have his or her needs met and therefore to secure the relevant primary goods. Criminogenic needs constitute the relevant deficits in the internal and external conditions.

There is a point in Ward and Maruna's assertion and that has to do with the importance of employment opportunity structures and the signaling considerations value of prison-based postsecondary education programs beyond their actual effects on offender recidivism rate considerations value (Cloward and Ohlin, 1960). The next thing to look at is the social considerations value of prison-based postsecondary education programs. The question, then, is what about them?

Social Considerations Value

Central to the social considerations value of postsecondary correctional education on prison-based education programs include but may not be limited to: (a) the social importance of prison-based college education programs, beyond their effects on offender recidivism; and (b) the recognition of the insight elimination of prison-based education Pell Grants in 1994 provides for our understanding of criminology, criminal justice, and public policy. Although these two themes are different, somehow, they interweave.

In 1994 Congress eliminated Pell Grants for prison-based postsecondary education programs in the United States, on the ground that the provision of educational programs for inmates in correctional institutions is not effective in achieving perceived goals measured in terms of recidivism rate (e.g., Denney and Tynes, 2021; Yates, 2012; Palmer, 2012; Tewksbury et al., 2000; Warner, 1999). However, as this book argues, education in prison is nonetheless valuable for several reasons other than their effects on offender recidivism (e.g., Schriro, 2012; Johnson, 2002; Petersilia, 2000; Hobler, 1999). To begin with, the value attached to education in the larger society as well as in prisons is strong. For instance, Welch (1996) asserts that correctional education programs continue to draw support from mainstream citizens essentially because in and of itself education is valued in our society in general. For one thing, educational and vocational programs do not only develop practical skills but also respond to the idea that any person has the right to be educated. They are probably our only hope for instilling and reinforcing a sense of the work ethic central to our culture's view of self-reliance, a satisfying life, and good citizenship (e.g., Denney and Tyne, 2021; Schriro, 2012; Sweetland, 1996).

Like education in the larger society, this idea of education in prison has some currency in the public arena, not only at the national level but also at the global level as mandated in the United Nations Declarations, Standards and Conventions as human rights for all people (Universal Declaration of Human Rights, 1948; UN Standard Minimum Rules for Treatment of Prisoners, 1955). Thus, former President Clinton states, "Education is the fault line, the great Continental Divide between those who will prosper and those who will not in the new economy" (Nicholas, 1996:14). This notion about the social considerations value of education was well stressed powerfully in Lejins's (1971:26) work, in which he asserts that:

> Since education is as good an indication as any of the likelihood of one's success in contemporary society, it seems essential to improve prison education programs if prison inmates are going to be provided with academic skills necessary to give them a realistic second chance at becoming constructive members in community life.

This claim about the social considerations value of education in prison in particular and the wider society in general becomes more compelling when one considers that about 95 percent of all offenders currently behind bars will eventually be released into the larger community where they will have to fend for themselves (Denney and Tynes, 2021; Bushway and Apel, 2012; Piquero, 2012; Visher et al., 2011; Lattimore et al., 2010; Travis, 2009; Petersilia, 2003). For example, Petersilia (2003:2) epitomizes this "iron law of imprisonment" (Travis, 2009) by asserting that:

> Inmates have always been released from prisons, and officials have long struggled with their reintegration. But the current situation is decidedly different. The sheer number of releasees dwarfs anything in history; the needs of parolees appear more serious; and the corrections system retains few rehabilitation programs.

Nonetheless, most research literature on the subject has suggested no simple connection between attainment of a correctional education program while incarcerated and successful reintegration into the larger community. However, it is the view of this author that the determination of the value of prison-based education programs is not and cannot be satisfactorily captured by one single measure of their usefulness or lack of it. Thus, the standard of recidivism rate reduction alone is shortsighted because for one thing it ignores other important considerations such as the social considerations value that would facilitate broader and deeper insights on the subject. Also, the standard of recidivism rate reduction only is one of the major factors that heighten the controversial debate of whether correctional education programs in our penal systems should continue to exist and be funded or not (e.g., Cullen et al., 2011; Ubah and Robinson, 2002; Martinson, 1974).

Another important social consideration value of prison education programs is that studies on the subject enable us to understand and appreciate how the developments or changes in the larger society (e.g., the elimination of prison-based education Pell Grants by Congress in 1994) affected prison-based college education programs and offender recidivism (Ubah, 2005). This understanding is important for sociology, criminology, criminal justice, and public policy alike because, all the technocratic language notwithstanding, it clearly shows how the life permitted to those inhabiting what Goffman (1961) describes as "total institutions" reflects the shifting values of society-at-large (e.g., Denney and Tynes, 2021; Delisi and Conis, 2013; Clear et al., 2013; Ubah, 2005; Ubah and Robinson, 2002; Farrington, 1992).

Thus, in his analysis, Goffman (1961:xiii) describes prisons as "places of residence and work where a large number of like-situated individuals, cut off from the wider society for an appreciable period of time, together lead an enclosed, formally administered round of life." But there is a point to this round, and it is a reflection of the larger society in which prisons are situated. In that sense, prisons can better be described as "organizations in action" (Ubah, 2014). Organizations in action are organizations that are in dynamic relationships with their environmental conditions and processes such as the political, legislative, judicial, economic, technological, and social milieu (e.g., Denney and Tynes, 2021; Ubah, 2014; Bushway and Apel, 2012; Farrington, 1992; Zucker, 1987; Aldrich and Pfeffer, 1976). As the loss of Pell Grants for prison-based college education programming in 1994 has shown, for instance, various external environmental forces and pressures can have profound negative effects on the internal social systems of a prison. On that note, what about the institutional function considerations value of prison-based education programs?

Institutional Function Considerations Value

Furthermore, in our efforts toward gaining further understanding and insights of some of the usefulness of prison-based education programs beyond their effects on offender recidivism rate is the institutional function considerations value of the programs. Thus, it has been documented that education programs in prison serve some important institutional functions such as job creation, control mechanism, and operational maintenance (e.g., Denney and Tynes, 2021; Austin, 2017; Pompoco et al., 2017; Wooldredge et al, 2017; Hunt and Dumville, 2016; Duwe et al., 2015; Lahm, 2009; French and Gendreau, 2006;

Johnson, 2002; Taylor and Tewksbury, 2002; Colvin, 1992; Langenbach et al., 1990; McKelvey, 1977).

The job creation value of education programs in prison serves an important institutional need in the sense that the programs provide jobs for some educators who may be employed to teach inmates in various academic and vocational fields. Some of these educators may come from within or outside correctional institutions. Some correctional institutions maintain viable education units and personnel for the provision of education needs for their institutions on a continuous basis which therefore provides gainful employment for a set of educators and their support groups. Some facilities also contract with other universities and colleges outside their institutions for the provision of education needs of their inmates, and sometimes facilities engage in a combination of the two depending on their needs (e.g., Denney and Tynes, 2021).

Perhaps more importantly, the programs may serve as control mechanisms and operational maintenance. This is so because the programs may serve as incentives which prison authorities can use to control inmates to conform to the rules and regulations of the penitentiary. For instance, access control to participation in educational programs as well as continuing participation in the programs provide prison authorities with a form of positive sanctions, which is crucial for maintaining order and reducing inmates' misconduct in prisons (Denney and Tynes, 2021; Austin, 2017; Wooldredge et al., 2017; Duwe et al., 2015; Clear et al., 2013; Lahm, 2009; French and Gendreau, 2006; Colvin, 1992; Langenbach, 1990).

In addition, programs may also serve the function of keeping inmates busy instead of being idle day in and day out. As is said, "An idle mind is the devil's workshop." And there is no place where this saying is more real and profound than in prison. This is so because prisoners must live within the walls of the institution. Experience has taught us that the more programs offered in prisons, the less idle inmates will be and the less likely that their idleness will translate into the devil's workshop. It is on this premise that correctional administrators use institutional programs to help manage inmate time. These programs help mitigate the oppressiveness and pain of doing time (Sykes, 1958; Garfinkel, 1956; Ubah, 2014). They also provide opportunities and hope for prisoners to improve their lives, no matter whether the programs involve counseling, religion, education, vocational training, or merely recreation. And they can change the culture of a facility in positive ways as well (e.g., Evans, 2019).

It has long been established that idleness is against the prevailing ethic. This Puritanism-derived ethic shapes most of our correctional ideologies and practices (e.g., Denney and Tynes, 2021; Austin, 2017; Delisi and Conis, 2019; Clear et al., 2013; Johnson, 2002; McKelvey, 1977). Thus, prison-based education programs may likely inhibit some crime and disorder in prison as well as offer a viable legitimate alternative for inmates who may be courageous and motivated enough to take advantage of the educational opportunity behind bars in their efforts toward turning their lives around which, in turn, could enable some of them to "go straight" by becoming productive citizens when released from the society of captives into the larger society (e.g., Vandala, 2019; Latessa, 2012; Maruna, 2012; Sykes, 1958).

Based on the above well-established facts, while conservative politicians, pessimistic ideologues, as well as the public seem concerned about tax dollars used to educate inmates, we should also realize that inmates' education has some crime preventive effects both within and outside the walls as well as other important functions than their effects on offender recidivism rate. As noted, the investment is a form of control mechanism, in that, without educational programs in prison to occupy inmates' time, alleviate the degree of prisonization and degradation ceremonies they go through (Clemmer, 1958; Garfinkel, 1956), and reinforce their motivation and hope to go straight, while at the same time controlling them in systematic ways, inmates are left to use their resources and imagination in nonproductive or counterproductive ways (e.g., Castro and Gould, 2019; Evans, 2018; Delisi and Conis, 2013; Dilulio, 1987; Taylor and Tewksbury, 2002).

LESSONS FOR 21ST CENTURY CRIMINOLOGY, CRIMINAL JUSTICE, AND PUBLIC POLICY: A SUMMARY

Several important lessons can be gleaned from this critical analysis. The first lesson is that there are other important considerations of the usefulness or lack of it of prison-based education programs beyond their intended effects on offender recidivism rate reduction. This lesson is very important because it is one of the major thrusts and distinctiveness of this book that prison-based education programs, especially at the postsecondary level, were not only meant to provide inmates with skills or credentials for recidivism rate reduction as they attempt to transition into the larger society, but also have other important values such as academic, employment signaling, institutional function, and social considerations (Clear, 2011; Maruna, 2012; Ubah, 2014).

That being the case, one of the challenges facing policy makers, correctional practitioners, scholars, and the public at large with regards to prison-based education programming is for all to be insightful enough about the other usefulness of prison-based education programs beyond their effects on offender recidivism rate. Recognizing and understanding the values of the considerations of the programs beyond their effects on offender recidivism rate could greatly aid stakeholders as they make critical decisions about whether the programs should continue to exist, and if so, how they should be structured and funded.

The second lesson that can be learned here is that it is important to recognize and understand that instead of the wasteful and pointless ways most prisoners do their time, we should instead encourage them to do their time constructively and maturely—by getting them to begin to better "think about stopping at red lights" as well as "learning their lessons" (Piquero, 2012; Johnson, 2002). Perhaps one of the important ways that could be accomplished is through a well-designed and well-funded postsecondary correctional education strategy that aims at mediating against offender's moral deficiency and delivers legitimate social skills and values. Such intervention programs could potentially enable some offenders to become more morally engaged in their everyday social actions and interactions. Such programs may also have the capacity to spur offenders to develop a belief in the law, obey the law, and thus become a productive member of society much more than before (Piquero, 2012; Wilkinson and Pickett, 2010; Jablecki, 2000).

As research suggests, inmates can learn their lessons constructively and maturely through prison-based education programs partially designed within the framework of the principles of "restorative justice" (e.g., Delisi and Conis, 2013; Sullivan and Tifft, 2005; Braithwaite and Strang, 2001; Halstead, 1999). For instance, Halstead (1999:42) argues that "restorative justice fits perfectly with the rehabilitative ideal because it concentrates on the harms of crime and corrections rather than the rules that have been broken."

Perhaps like the approach of this book, the principles of restorative justice go beyond the status quo upon which most of our criminal justice system programs are currently based to an idea and philosophy that would help us in the attempts toward addressing the problems of crime and penal systems for the betterment of the victims, offenders, and the general public (e.g., Braithwaite and Strang, 2001). This philosophy is based on the premise of showing inmates how they are responsible for the consequences of their choices.

Unfortunately, most of the studies on the subject are mainly concerned with the debate over whether prison-based education programs work or do not work as measured by offender recidivism rate, while to a great degree, they ignored the need to give adequate attention to academic, employment signaling, institutional function, and social considerations values of the programs. In this manuscript, however, this author has made serious efforts to make an explicit and compelling case for the other important considerations value of prison-based education programs other than recidivism rate, and in the process has gleaned some lessons and gained some deep insights as well as recognized some of the importance of such lessons and insights for criminology, criminal justice, public policy, and the public in general. In the final analysis, it must be reemphasized that the usefulness of correctional education programs cannot be satisfactorily captured by using offender recidivism rate as the only measure. Multiple criteria other than only recidivism rate are imperative and highly desirable steps in 21st century criminology, criminal justice, and corrections policy and administration.

Chapter 7

The History of Pell Grants for Prison Inmate College Education

INTRODUCTION

Prison-based college education programs started long before the establishment of federal grants for prison-based postsecondary education. According to history, the first recorded college education program for inmates was established by Southern Illinois University at Carbondale at the Menard Correctional Center in Illinois in 1948 (Matisoff, 1973). Because this chapter is focusing on the history of Pell Grants for prison-based education, not much will be said about the pioneering college education program for inmates at Menard Correctional Center in Illinois. Instead, the chapter will focus on the history of prison-based education Pell Grants. It can be said that the history of Pell Grants for prison inmate postsecondary education began in 1965 when the program was established by Congress through the passage of the Higher Education Act of 1965 during the presidency of Lyndon Johnson. In this chapter, we will focus mainly on the early history of Pell Grants for prison inmates' postsecondary education and the rationale for the grants. But the other aspects of the program, especially its abolition in 1994 by Congress during the speakership of Newt Gingrich—a former congressman from the state of Georgia—will be discussed in detail in the chapter that follows.

EARLY HISTORY OF PELL GRANTS FOR PRISON-BASED COLLEGE EDUCATION

Prison inmate college education Pell Grants was part and parcel of Pell Grants for the general society. The federal Pell Grant program used to be known as the Basic Education Opportunity Grants, a bill of rights for G.I. Joe and G.I. Jane (the G.I. Bill), the Educational Development Program, the Manpower Development and Training Act, and Voc. Rehab. Most of these grants were originally established for World War II veterans, beginning in 1944. In 1965 Congress passed the Higher Education Act, which extended guaranteed student loans to anyone attending a postsecondary education program, provided the person is qualified for it (Wood, 1997). The act was an integral part of President Johnson's grand initiatives or agenda: the "great society" programs (Robinson and English, 2017; Delisi and Conis, 2014; McCarthy et al., 2001). But the most important aspect of the act for the purposes of this book is Title IV in the 1965 Higher Education Act, which explicitly permitted inmates to apply for financial aid for postsecondary education (Center on Crime, Community and Culture, 1997). The grants collectively became known as Pell Grants, in part because of the role Rhode Island's U.S. Senator Claiborne Pell played in the efforts to save the grants from elimination by conservative lawmakers in the U.S. Senate. In addition to the tireless role played by Senator Pell in the efforts to save the grants, other liberal law makers (especially Senators Bayh and Metzenbaum) also fought greatly to keep the programs.

Senator Pell was so active in the campaign to keep the programs from elimination that in 1977 the programs were renamed in his honor. Until the complete elimination of Pell Grants for inmate college education in 1994 by the United States Congress, Pell Grants were the primary sources of funding for postsecondary correctional education projects in America.

RATIONALE FOR PRISON INMATE COLLEGE EDUCATION PELL GRANTS

As noted above, federal Pell Grants were extended to prison inmates in America for postsecondary education through Title IV in the 1965 Higher Education Act during the presidency of Lyndon Johnson (Center on Crime, Community and Culture, 1997). The grants were to be used to subsidizing college education costs for students from low-income families. These funds enabled inmates interested in attending a college correctional education program but unable to afford the costs of enrollment. Like federal college Pell Grants for students in the general society, prison-based Pell Grants were non-repayable because their recipients were men and women from low-income families. Because most incarcerated men and women come from low-income families, Pell Grants became the primary source of funding for prison inmate college education programming across the United States (Robinson and English, 2017; Gehring, 1997; Ubah, 2001).

The prison inmate postsecondary education Pell Grants program was designed under the purview that it will enable some incarcerated men and women to get a college education, which they did not have the opportunity to do prior to their incarceration. This idea emanated from the notion that acquiring college educational credentials while in prison would provide inmates with legitimate human capital (resources that influence future activities in people). Human capital such as marketable labor skills and trades can equip inmates for better job opportunities, which in turn could build social bonds that protect against criminal behavior as well as help enhance their families and communities (e.g., Denney and Tynes, 2021; Becker, 1964; Febero and Schwartz, 1995; Hershberger, 1987; Palmer, 1992; Pendleton, 1988; Robinson and English, 2017; Sweetland, 1996; Tootoonchi, 1990).

Generally, education is viewed as an equalizer of opportunities. Indeed, it has been documented that going to college enables one to obtain credentials for the labor market that could open considerable opportunities for social mobility (Ellis and Lane, 1963). Thus, "The higher the attainment of education, the greater one's earning power and the greater the possibility of improving one's station in life" (Johnson, 1964:610). This assumption suggests that inmates' completion of, or participation in, a college correctional education program with the aid of Pell Grant funding is evidence of their being engaged in the process of upward mobility. This is because such a program provides inmates with the necessary human capital resources (skills and knowledge) that can help some of them to "go straight" and abandon criminal behavior when released.

As Denney and Tynes (2021), Nicholas (1996), and Hershberger (1987), among others, have stressed persuasively, inmates' educational successes in prison seem to have a generalizing effect because they tend to prepare ex-offenders to further their education elsewhere. Through correctional education, inmates should find the motivation to go on in their educational experience, and they may be able to improve their chances of staying out of prison after completing some courses.

With the above well-informed views, the optimistic theorists suggest that the idea of Pell Grants for a prison inmate college education program is the right step in the right direction because the program can promote change in some inmates, improve their psychological well-being, and offer them credentials for the labor market. The premise of the idealistic theories form the arsenal from which proponents of correctional education programs draw their arguments for the continuing provision and funding of Pell Grants for prison inmate college education programs.

SUMMARY

Prison-based Pell Grants for college education programs started with the passage of the 1965 Higher Education Act during the Presidency of Lyndon Johnson. It was Title IV in the 1965 Higher Education Act that explicitly permitted inmates to apply for financial aid for postsecondary education. The grants were initially known by other names, but they eventually became known as Pell Grants because of the role Rhode Island's U.S. Senator Claiborne Pell played in the efforts to save the grants from elimination by conservative lawmakers in the U.S. Senate. Like federal college Pell Grants for students in the general society, prison-based Pell Grants were used to subsidize college education costs for students from low-income families. And because most incarcerated men and women come from low-income families, Pell Grants became the primary sources of funding for prison inmate college education programming across the United States. However, in 1994 Pell Grants for prison inmate postsecondary education were abolished by Congress during the speakership of Newt Gingrich, who was then representing the state of Georgia in Congress.

Chapter 8

Abolition of Pell Grants for Higher Education of Prisoners

INTRODUCTION

The rehabilitative and reintegrative correctional philosophies see prison inmate college education as an effective approach to the reduction of offender recidivism rate. The provision of prison-based college education Pell Grants by Congress were part and parcel of these correctional philosophies. From its inception in 1965, prison-based Pell Grants were the primary sources of funding for inmate college education across all states and correctional institutions in the United States until the program was abolished by Congress in 1994 (e.g., Robinson and English, 2017; Ubah, 2004; Batiuk, 1997; Tewksbury and Taylor, 1996; Zook, 1994).

The debate over the abolition of Pell Grants for prison inmate postsecondary education is captured in two contradictory perspectives: (a) an idealistic view stressing the program's promise and value: and (b) a pessimistic reaction to its existence (e.g., Ubah and Ubah, 2019). These two contradictory perspectives on the debate over the elimination of prison-based education Pell Grants are captured in the political contexts of the issue. The abolition of Pell Grants for prison inmate college education in the United States in 1994 was not without enormous consequences. In this chapter, adequate efforts are made to discuss the political process that led to the elimination of Pell Grants for the college-in-prison inmate education program, the consequences of the abolition, and the Second Chance Pell Pilot program that seems to have ended the abolition of Pell Grants for prison-based college education.

THE POLITICAL CONTEXT OF PRISON-BASED EDUCATION PELL GRANTS

Political considerations and impacts on correctional systems are not new (e.g., Delisi and Conis, 2019; Brown and Philo, 2017; Davidson, 1997; McKelvey, 1977). For example, Davidson (1997:136) asserts that "throughout the 19th century and early 20th, prison reformers attributed many of their setbacks to political interferences. The 1992 and 1994 congressional assault on Pell Grants for prison higher education programs would suggest that politics continues to be a problem." Thus, it was evident by the late 1970s and early 1980s that there was a clear political threat to inmate access to Pell Grant education funding (Gehring, 1997). The move to eliminate Pell Grants, in the form of a federal crime bill, was introduced to the senate by Senator Kay Bailey Hutchinson, a Texas Republican. However, adherents and opponents of the bill cut across party lines (Robinson and English, 2017; Zook, 1994).

Each year, during 1982–1994, conservative lawmakers in Congress introduced bills to cut back Pell Grants for inmate students. Each bill was defeated, but the efforts had a cumulative impact on the campaign to eliminate the grants. The long-maintained effort finally achieved its goal partially in 1992 when the Higher Education Act (HEA) of 1965 was amended, prohibiting prisoners serving a sentence of life without parole or sentenced to death from receiving Pell Grants, and completely abolished in 1994 when prison inmate eligibility for Pell Grant educational funding was fully eliminated by the "tough on crime" Congress during the speakership of Newt Gingrich, a former congressman from the state of Georgia that passed the 1993 Violent Crime Control and Law Enforcement Act and the Higher Education Reauthorization Act of 1994 (Robinson and English, 2017; Batiuk, 1997; Davidson, 1997; Tewksbury and Taylor, 1996). The 1994 law stated:

> Section 401(b)(8) of the Higher Education Act of 1965 (20 U.S.C. 1070a(b)(8) is amended to read as follows: (8) No basic grant shall be awarded under this subpart to any individual who is incarcerated in any Federal or state penal institution.

With the elimination of inmate access to Pell monies by Congress, prisoners were excluded from the centuries-old American enterprise of mass education until in 2007 when President George W. Bush signed the Second Chance Act which amended the ban and partially granted prisons access to federal funding for various rehabilitation and reentry initiatives including that tertiary education programs might now receive federal funding once again for prison-based postsecondary education (e.g., Denney and Tynes, 2021; Bannin, 2021; Robinson and English, 2017).

It is important to note that efforts to eliminate prison-based Pell Grants in 1994 were much encouraged by the partisan interpretations of Martinson's (1974) article by the critics of correctional education programming (e.g., Denney and Tynes, 2021; Mario and Guy, 2014; Gehring, 1997; Gendreau, 1996). Perhaps it is even more important to note that the most definitive pessimistic reaction literature challenging the idealistic view of rehabilitative programs in prisons is the survey by Lipton, Martinson, and Wilks (1975) of the results of prison reform programs for adult men offenders between 1945 and 1967. From this survey, Martinson (1974) spun off a controversial article in which he assessed several rehabilitative studies to answer the general question of "what works?" in prison reform. He analyzed several studies that support the notion that rehabilitative programs do not work, as well as others that support the position that rehabilitative programs are effective. In addition, he criticized those studies that appeared not to support the pessimistic view of the usefulness of rehabilitative programs as measured by recidivism rates. He did so by charging those studies with producing no clear pattern to indicate the efficacy of any method of treatment and summarized his findings by concluding that "with few and isolated exceptions, the rehabilitative efforts that have been reported so far have had no appreciable effects on recidivism" (Martinson, 1974:25).

Martinson's article was titled "What Works? Questions and Answers about Prison Reform," but it was quickly interpreted and became known as the "nothing works" report (Latessa et al., 2015; Welch, 1996). The conclusion that "nothing works" had considerable impact on the academic and political discussion of inmate rehabilitative programs. Critics of the rehabilitative ideal embraced eagerly the "nothing works" verdict to help justify abandoning rehabilitation and redirecting American correctional philosophy and practice to the new epoch of deterrence and incapacitation (Mario and Guy, 2014; Ubah, 2014; Delisi and Conis, 2019; Davidson, 1997; Stevens and Ward, 1997; Gendreau, 1996).

It is important to note that contrary to popular opinion, Lipton, Martinson, and Wilks (1975) did not make the sweeping claim that "nothing works." Rather, they cited positive outcomes in 48 percent of the programs evaluated. The question then is, how can one describe Martinson's sweeping conclusion as "nothing works" when some things really did work? (Latessa et al., 2015).

The author suggests that Martinson's "nothing works" conclusion regarding rehabilitative efforts on corrections was a "carnival mirror" image conclusion concerning the results of rehabilitative efforts. A carnival mirror is a mirror that hides as much as it reveals—a mirror that distorts the true image of the picture shown (Reiman and Leighton, 2017). It is a carnival mirror conclusion in the sense that Martinson's conclusion did not show the complete picture of correctional rehabilitation efforts. By focusing mainly on the dark and giving little or no attention to the encouraging side of the entire picture, the "nothing works" conclusion distorted and continues to distort the image of the results of offender rehabilitation efforts up to the present time, in that the "nothing works" rhetoric and conclusion are usually the major basis of argument and reference point for critics of offender rehabilitation (Austin, 2017; Berghuis, 2018).

Perhaps it is equally important to note that Martinson (1979) revisited some of his earlier conclusions on offender rehabilitation, and he came to somewhat different conclusions from his earlier assessment. He reported that some rehabilitative programs were indeed beneficial and that some treatment programs did have an appreciable effect on recidivism (Latessa et al., 2015). Yet Martinson's later (partial) change of mind received little attention compared with the splash made by his earlier evaluation. Thus, "It is ironic, but instructive, that whereas Martinson's 1974 'nothing works' article is among the most cited criminological writings, his revisionist 1979 essay earned scant attention" (Welch, 1996:100). One is tempted to conclude that the later position "failed" while the earlier one "succeeded," not because of the demerits of the revised argument, but because of its failure to be in tune with a climate of opinion increasingly frustrated with and hostile to a rehabilitative ideal (Austin, 2017; Paparozzi and Guy, 2014).

As one would expect, Martinson's (1974) study is not without critics of its own. For example, Palmer (1975) argues that Martinson's study is characterized by bias, inconsistency, and omission of facts, regarding the somewhat optimistic assessment of intensive supervision programs that have provided the most encouraging reports on offender rehabilitation. Palmer notes that throughout Martinson's correctional education assessment, he was most interested in assessing the total efficacy of each given prison-based education program as the sum of a program's effects on all the variables that had been studied. Palmer concludes that this criterion of a universally effective program was "a search for the impossible." In other words, it was designed to fail (Reiman and Leighton, 2017).

Even though some studies may have shed useful insights on the interacting processes that shape the negative interpretations of Martinson's (1974) work. The author thinks that Cullen and Gendreau (1989:24) probably provided the more useful perspective for an understanding of the idiosyncrasies underlying the negative interpretations of Martinson's work, by suggesting that "the rejection of rehabilitation has less to do with a careful reading of empirical literature and more to do with changes in the social fabric that triggered a corresponding shift in thinking about corrections." Perhaps there is no better indication of the change perceived by Cullen and Gendreau than the elimination of prison-based education Pell Grants in 1994 by a Republican-led Congress until 2007, as will be demonstrated below.

It cannot be overemphasized that efforts to eliminate prison-based Pell Grants were much encouraged by the partisan interpretations of Martinson's (1974) article by the critics of correctional education program (e.g., Mario and Guy, 2014; Gehring, 1997; Gendreau, 1996). A close look at the negative interpretations of Martinson's conclusion on offender rehabilitation suggests their political implications. This is because they show an affinity with the position of political conservatives who wanted to get rid of, or cripple, the domination of offender rehabilitative ideologies, and to replace them instead with their own ideologies for the treatment of offenders as evildoers of society who are supposed to be punished and deterred through determinate and harsh sentences and not prison-based postsecondary programs (Delisi and Conis, 2014; Morphonios and Wilson, 1991). Thus, Cullen and Gendreau (1989:26) observed that:

> It is helpful to view these developments in the context of important social changes transpiring in the 1970s. The nation was struggling to reassemble the role of strong government after the turbulent 1960s, and one method of achieving this goal was to mount a visible tough-on-crime campaign. The tough-on-crime ideology asserted that those who favored rehabilitation were `bleeding heart' liberals—suggesting that liberals were soft on crime.

There is evidence indicating that the tough-on-crime ideologues did succeed in their political agenda to a great extent. This is partly attributable to the fact that Martinson's (1974) "nothing works" verdict on offender rehabilitation added scientific respectability, and its resonance could be felt in the shift in the ideology of corrections and approaches from more emphasis on treatment/rehabilitation to more emphasis on incapacitation/justice orientation (Denney and Tynes, 2021; Latessa et al., 2015; Delisi and Conis, 2014; Paparozzi and Guy, 2014; Jancic, 1998; Stevens and Ward, 1997). In the same vein, the negative interpretation of Martinson's work also offered critics of rehabilitation programs an opportunity to argue for financial cutbacks or complete eradication of prison-based Pell Grants funding. When they succeeded in this agenda in 1994, the impacts of their efforts did not stop.

ELIMINATION OF PRISON-BASED PELL GRANTS: THE CONSEQUENCES

As Tewksbury and Taylor (1996) observed, somewhat tendentiously, the elimination of Pell Grants for inmate educational projects was an indication that voters and legislators around the country had chosen inmates' recidivism over inmates' rehabilitation and successful reintegration into the larger society. This is evidenced by the fact that subsequent reductions have cut even deeper into inmate education in general and postsecondary correctional programs.

The elimination of Pell Grants led to cutbacks in funding for most of the correctional rehabilitative programs in the United States. As a result, most prison-based postsecondary education programs in most states were completely phased out of existence due to lack of funds (Denney and Tynes, 2021; Latessa at el., 2015; Ubah, 2001; Petersilia, 2000; Tewksbury and Taylor, 1996). According to the Center on Crime, Community and Culture (1997), the elimination of Pell monies for correctional education has forced more than one-half of correctional institutions in each state to make cuts over the five years preceding its report in their inmate education budgets, with some jurisdictions eliminating such programs entirely.

Research shows a widespread agreement by wardens and directors of correctional education programs across the nation of the adverse impact of the end of inmate education Pell Grants. The magnitude of the effects of the cuts in inmate education became evident in the results of the assessment by Tewksbury and Taylor (1996:62). According to them:

> The elimination of Pell Grants funding for incarcerated students in 1994 has had a profound effect on post-secondary correctional education programming throughout the nation. In 1 year, the number of correctional systems offering PSCE programs dropped from 82.6 percent (N = 38) in 1994–95 to 63 percent (29) in 1995–96. Naturally, the range of program options decreased as well. Whereas in 1994–95, 52 percent of systems offered certificate programs, 71 percent associate degrees, 48 percent baccalaureate degrees, and 13 percent graduate programs, by 1995–96 the numbers had decreased to 39 percent of systems offering certificate programs, 50 percent associate degrees, 33 percent baccalaureates, and only 6 percent graduate degree programs.

As a result of the elimination of Pell monies, nearly 41 percent of correctional education directors reported the elimination had "completely changed" their programs, whereas only 18 percent of correctional systems reported no changes. If the critics of the rehabilitative approach to incarceration are correct, these changes should have little, if any, impact on the number or magnitude of offender recidivism. Unfortunately for them, empirical literature has shown that the changes had negative impact on the number of offender recidivists in most of the state correctional systems that experienced the changes (Crow and Smykla, 2014; Latessa at el., 2015; Ubah, 2001).

While the elimination of Pell Grants has been a disaster nationally for prison-based college education programs, some few states, such as Ohio, Maryland, Delaware, New York, and Illinois, seem to have been able to adapt to their loss much better than most states in the union. For example, these states have been able to find new revenue sources that enabled them to move against the trend and continue to support educational opportunities for inmates (Batiuk, 1997; Hobler, 1999; Tracy et al., 1998). The three remaining ways through which inmates can pay for their college education include Federal Perkins Funds, private funds (their own or those of family members), and state-based education grants (Tewksbury and Taylor, 1996). In the state of Illinois, for instance, state-based education grants are more widely used by inmates than other funding alternatives (Ubah, 2001).

It is important to note that even though the elimination of prison-based Pell Grants had serious profound negative impacts on correctional education programming in the United States, it would be shortsighted to attribute total responsibility to external social factors. Internal factors also play a part in the demise of prison-based schooling in many institutions. Some of these factors have been identified as the confused professional identity issue and the status position of the "good old boys" (GOBs) within the United States penal systems (Seashore and Haberfield, 1976; Gehring, 1997).

The issue of confused professional identity suggests that many correctional educators are not enthusiastic and supportive of higher education for inmates. Most correctional educators do not identify with their field, instead they identify with another field of education or with security or administration at their institution. Only about 10 percent of correctional educators in the United States are members of the Correctional Education Association, irrespective of the fact that the association is the backbone of education in correctional institutions in the United States (Seashore and Haberfield, 1997).

Just like most bureaucratic organizations across the globe, the status positions of the good GOBs in correctional institutions in the United States sometimes impose some problem for correctional education programs. This is because most correctional education programs are managed by GOBs. It has been suggested that these GOBs, instead of focusing more attention on the advancement of student learning, are sometimes more interested in using the programs as instruments for bringing in revenue to their institutions, advancing a personal career, and/or getting a "soft money" position shifted to a tenure track (Gehring, 1997).

SUMMARY

Rehabilitative and reintegrative correctional philosophies see prison inmate college education as an effective approach to reduction of the offender recidivism rate. The provision of prison-based college education Pell Grants by Congress was part and parcel of these correctional philosophies. However, prison-based Pell Grants for inmate college education across all states' correctional institutions in the United States was abolished by Congress in 1994 and reinstated in 2007 and 2015 respectively. This chapter critically and rigorously examined the political process that led to the abolition of Pell Grants for prison inmates' college education in the United States and the consequences of the abolition. However, with the emergence of the Second Chance Act and the Second Chance Pell Pilot programs, there seems to be an eventual end of the abolition of Pell monies for prison-based postsecondary education programs to which we now turn.

Chapter 9

Second Chance Act and Second Chance Pell Pilot Program

The End of Abolition of Pell Grants for Prisoner Education

INTRODUCTION

As noted in chapter 8, in 1994 prison inmate eligibility for Pell Grant postsecondary education program funding was eliminated by the "tough on crime" U.S. Congress, which passed the 1993 Violent Crime Control and Law Enforcement Act and the Higher Education Reauthorization Act of 1994 (Batiuk, 1997; Davidson, 1997; Tewksbury and Taylor, 1996). The elimination had profound negative consequences in the provision and delivery of postsecondary correctional education programs across the United States (Denney and Tynes, 2021; Robinson and English, 2017; Latessa at el., 2015; Ubah, 2001; Petersilia, 2000; Center on Crime, Community and Culture, 1997; Tewksbury and Taylor, 1996). For example, research shows that the elimination of Pell Grants led to cutbacks in the funding for most of the correctional rehabilitative programs in the United States. As a result, most prison-based postsecondary education programs in most states were completely phased out due to lack of funds (Denney and Tynes, 2021; Latessa at el., 2015; Ubah, 2001; Petersilia, 2000; Tewksbury and Taylor, 1996). However, there seems to be an eventual end of the abolition of Pell monies for college-in-prison education programs. How? The answers to the question lie with review of the Second Chance Act and the Second Chance Pell Pilot Program, to which we now turn.

THE SECOND CHANCE ACT

In 2007 President George W. Bush signed into law the Second Chance Act (SCA) which encompasses key elements of the successful Prisoner Reentry Initiative (PRI) he announced during his 2004 State of the Union address to help released prisoners successfully reintegrate into the community (Robinson and English, 2017; White House Office of the Press Secretary, 2008). The SCA formally amended the ban on prison access to federal funding for rehabilitation and reintegration programs and partially granted prisons access to federal funding for various rehabilitation and reentry initiatives. The access included that tertiary education programs might now again receive federal funding for various prisoner reentry programs. The funding and administration of the SCA are handled by the U.S Department of Justice's Office of Justice Programs. Specifically, the Bureau of Justice Assistance oversees the adult aspect of the grants whereas the Office of Juvenile Justice and Delinquency Prevention handles the juvenile aspect of the grants (Bureau of Justice Assistance Fact Sheet, 2022).

But the implementation of Bush's Second Chance Act focuses mostly on community-based prisoner reentry programs by enhancing drug treatment, mentoring, and transitional services for ex-inmates through partnership with various stakeholders including but not limited to local corrections agencies and faith-based and community organizations. But, by signing the Second Chance Act into law, Bush formally laid the foundation for reinstating Pell Grants federal funding for prison-based postsecondary education in the United States.

THE SECOND CHANCE PELL PILOT PROGRAM

Following President Bush's footsteps on laudable correctional reform-oriented initiative, President Obama built upon the foundation laid by Bush's Second Chance Act, and among other things, formally reinstated Pell Grants federal funding for prison-based postsecondary education programs through the Second Chance Pell Pilot Initiative in 2015. This approach was part and parcel of President Obama's broader criminal justice system reform agenda (Burger et al., 2022; Bannin, 2021; Denney and Tynes, 2021; Robinson and English, 2017; Martin, 2016; White House Office of the Press Secretary, 2015).

There are three major factors that bolster support for the establishment of the Second Chance Pell Pilot Initiative. The first was the renewed push by governors to reform their costly prison systems as part of their approach in responding to and managing the unusual challenging economic environment during the Obama administration (Delisi and Conis, 2019; Robinson and English, 2017).

The second factor was the steadfast growth and success of university-sponsored prison education programs that continued or began after the elimination of college-in-prison Pell Grant federal funding in 1994 to provide postsecondary classes for inmates for free or for a modest financial cost. Notable examples of such universities and colleges include the Prison University Project in California, the Cornell Prison Education Project, and especially the Bard Prison Initiative in New York, which created a Consortium for the Liberal Arts college education in prison. As of 2021, fourteen college programs were part of the consortium which spread across ten states. They include the University of Notre Dame and Holy Cross College, Wesleyan University, Goucher College, Washington University in St. Louis, Grinnell College, Boston College, Bennington College, Emerson College, and Yale University, among others (Denney and Tynes, 2021; Emery, 2020; National Humanities Medal, 2015; Robinson and English, 2017).

The third factor was empirical evidence from the evaluation of prison-based education programs (postsecondary and others), especially the one conducted by the Rand Corporation (Davis et al., 2013; Hall, 2015; RAND Corporation, 2019) which revealed that the programs made a significant difference both in the reduction of recidivism and the cost effectiveness of the programs. Findings of the study show strong and clear evidence of large and statistically significant reduction of the risk of recidivism of 43 percent following participation in both the basic education and postsecondary correctional programs. Findings of the study also show that every dollar invested in correctional educational programming resulted in a \$4–\$5 return from savings generated by reduced reincarceration costs (e.g., Delisi and Conis, 2019; Denney and Tynes, 2021; Davis et al., 2013; Hall, 2015; Duwe, 2017; Fogarty and Giles, 2018; Robinson and English, 2017).

These findings of the studies provided both the academic and cost-effectiveness records of evidence of successful prison-based postsecondary education programs for the Obama administration as they announced the Second Chance Pell Pilot Program in July 2015 as an Experimental Sites Initiative authorized under 487(b) of the Higher Education Act of 1965 (Department of Corrections Staff, 2019; Delisi and Conis, 2019; Robinson and English, 2017; White House Office of the Press Secretary, 2015; Wood, 1997). The Second Chance Pell Pilot Program was designed to test whether giving incarcerated individuals access to Pell Grants federal funding for higher education increases their participation in postsecondary education programs and influences their academic and life outcomes. The pilot programs began on June 24, 2016, when the Department of Education announced the selection of about 67 schools across 26 states to participate in the program, with the participating schools working with a selected number of corrections facilities and other stakeholders to enroll qualified prison inmates in the pilots.

The initiative provided postsecondary education opportunity for some inmates at any of the designated sites provided they were interested in participating in the program and qualified for it as determined by prison administrators. The sites were chosen based on institutional diversity, including location, institution types, Title IV participation level, and enrollment (Denney and Tynes, 2021; Karpowitz, 2017; Robinson and English, 2017). During the pilot's first two years of operation schools awarded approximately $35.6 million Pell grants to about 8,800 prison inmates (Department of Corrections Staff, 2019). The date the Second Chance Pell Pilot Initiative would end has not been announced by the Department of Education, which has noted that experiments under the initiative typically run up to three to four years.

However, in 2018 the Second Chance Act was reauthorized, and a new set of federal grants was awarded to support education and employment reentry program strategies in 28 states and jurisdictions across the country. Three examples of the current SCA initiatives are: Adult Reentry and Employment Strategies Planning Program of FY 2018; Correctional Adult Reentry Education, Employment, and Recidivism Reduction Strategies Program (CAREERRS) of FY 2020; and Adult Reentry Education, Employment, Treatment, and Recovery Program of 2021 (Bureau of Justice Assistance, 2022).

Evaluation research that would assess whether the experiments had any significant effects on the recidivism rates of inmates who participated in the programs is necessary because knowledge of the outcomes of the initiatives is important for criminology, criminal justice, public policy, and the public in general for various reasons. Among them include but are not limited to the fact that offender rehabilitation is one of the goals of the correctional system and a very controversial one that continues to divide policy makers, correctional practitioners, scholars, and the public. Therefore, such knowledge would, among other things, enable us to have broader and deeper insights and understanding of the academic debate over prison-based education programs and offender recidivism. It will aid policy makers and correctional administrators in making critical decisions about whether the initiatives should continue to exist and, if so, how they should be structured, administered, and funded. It will aid policy makers and correctional administrators in identifying effective and viable rehabilitative programs. And it will assist correctional administrators in identifying variables that serve as predictors of inmate success in the programs and predictors of successful program utilization (e.g., Denney and Tynes, 2021; Robinson, 1990).

Without such knowledge on recidivism, it is impossible to compare the efficacy of the initiatives among other correctional agencies and institutions that were not part of the initiatives. With the knowledge, it becomes feasible to focus attention upon those initiatives and other institutions which appear to have the greatest salutary effects upon the offenders whom they reach. It would help send signals to employers as they make employment decisions on whether or not to hire an ex-offender. And it will give deeper and broader insights on some of the social issues concerning prison-based education programs and offender recidivism rates. Therefore, it can be concluded that the knowledge from the initiatives on recidivism would provide lessons that may be too important and too costly to ignore in 21st century criminology, criminal justice, public policy, and corrections management and practice (Bannin, 2021; Denney and Tynes, 2021; Ubah, 2019; Drake and Fumia, 2017; Bushway and Apel, 2013; Robinson, 1990; Mandel, 1963).

Nonetheless, the experiments were not without some challenges of their own which seem to limit their smooth operations. Those challenges include but may not be limited to the difficulties in establishing incarcerated applicants' eligibility for Pell Grants as some applicants were not registered for selective service, and some had existing federal student loan in default. Second is the challenges many incarcerated applicants face as they attempt to obtain documents to support verification of their applications that would enable the Department of Education to avoid inappropriate payment of federal financial aid. And the third challenge is providing new processes and creative solutions in the efforts to overcome inherent technological limitations, space limitations, and the transfer of students to other institutions before the completion of the program they enrolled in (Delisi and Conis, 2019; Department of Corrections Staff, 2019; United States Government Accountability Office, 2019; Osborne, 2019; RAND Corporation, 2019).

SUMMARY

It is a well-established fact that prisons are "organizations in action" (Ubah, 2014; Farrington, 1992). An organization in action is one that is in dynamic relationship with its environmental processes and changes such as political, legislative, judicial, economic, technological, academic, and social milieu (e.g., Delisi and Conis, 2019; Ubah, 2014; Bushway and Apel, 2012; Farrington, 1992; Zucker, 1987). For instance, as the abolition in 1994 of Pell Grants by Congress for college correctional education programs—as well as the eventual end of the abolition with the emergence of the Second Chance Act in 2007 and the Second Chance Pell Pilot Initiative in 2015—has shown, various environmental forces and pressures can have profound negative and/or positive effects on the internal social systems of a prison.

This is so as those political developments and climates have clearly demonstrated. As a result, this chapter makes serious efforts in examining and analyzing the political process that led to the end of the abolition of Pell Grants for prison inmates' college education in the United States which occurred in the form of the Second Chance Act and the Second Chance Pell Pilot Initiative. These two major acts of political development and/or change have once again made available Pell monies for prison-based college education programs in the country, at least partially and for now.

As the author observes tendentiously, some of the major lessons that can be learned and the deep insights that can be gleaned with the above identified political developments and changes are that they suggest in part or in whole that our contemporary prisons may be better understood with structural functional approach or open systems perspective instead of the total institution theory advocated by Goffman (e.g., Delisi and Conis, 2019; Ubah, 2014; Bastedo, 2004; Scott, 2002; Goffman, 1961). To be clear, structural functional approach or open systems perspective is a view of a social system such as prisons as fluid, therefore interacting with their environmental forces and pressures (e.g., Bushway and Apel, 2012; Bastedo, 2004; Farrington, 1992). Therefore, it is important to note that structural functional approach or open systems perspective is embedded in the concept of prisons as organizations in action (Ubah, 1914).

Chapter 10

Limitations, Direction for Future Research, and Conclusion

INTRODUCTION

This chapter presents the limitations of the book and offers some direction for future research on offender rehabilitation issues, as well as draws some conclusions. The chapter presents the fruits of previous chapters of the book, which include the constraints encountered, the major lessons learned, the deeper insights gleaned, and offers some direction for future research on some of the issues emanating from the manuscript. In important ways, the chapter reminds us that we should always endeavor to engage ourselves and our minds in the process of consistently examining and reexamining our social realities no matter how good or bad they may seem at a particular time and place. With that approach as a toolkit, this chapter makes serious efforts to discuss the limitations and conclusions of the book and suggests some directions that may be plausible for future research.

LIMITATIONS

It is important to caution about some of the limitations of this study because, among other things, such information could provide important lessons and insights that would enable us to be better informed about the shortcomings of the study. Also, such knowledge can be very valuable for future systematic research and practice. Therefore, what follows are the limitations of this book. They include but may not be limited to the following:

First, this book is limited to issues involving correctional-education programs and the offender recidivism rate. A prison-based education program is a very significant aspect of offender rehabilitative programs. This means that other aspects of offender rehabilitative programs, such as counseling, religion, anger management, and community-based programs, were not included in the book. This approach was employed to keep the focus of the book appropriately narrowed to the prison-based correctional-educational aspect of offender rehabilitation, so that it wouldn't be too ambitious like the generality of focus employed by Martinson's (1974) controversial survey which assessed the literature on various aspects of offender rehabilitative programs published between 1945 and 1967. Martinson examined both prison-based rehabilitative literature and community-based programs and included correctional education studies, offender counseling studies, medical treatment studies, deincarceration studies, et al. The excessive broadness of the approach used by Martinson is one of the aspects of his report that had been criticized heavily by several scholars (e.g., Palmer, 1975; Reiman, 1995; Welch, 1996; Ubah, 2002).

Second, the aspects of correctional education programs specifically focused on here are the postsecondary ones rather than the GED courses and programs. In part, the reason for this is that participation in GED courses is mandatory; thus, there is no nonparticipating comparison group that would allow an estimate of education's impact on offender recidivism rates. Secondly, if any correctional education programming will be a significant recidivism reducer, college-level educational programming is the most likely one. As Ubah (2002:18) epitomizes in his study that "education should not be viewed as some uniform and homogenous entity exposure to which gives skills and alters thinking and motivation invariably in the same fashion." In part, this is so because the credentials inmates might acquire by participating in prison-based postsecondary education programs increase human capital (resources that increase saleable abilities in people, such as marketable skills and trades) much more than GED programs do (Denney and Tynes, 2021; Ubah, 2014).

Third, different measurements of recidivism were identified and analyzed in this book. Some of the measurements of recidivism are seriously limited in their utility. Examples of such measures include the use of rearrest and reconviction as determination of recidivism. This is so because those measures of recidivism are not rigorous enough to be capable of meeting all the appropriate layers involved in the process of reincarceration of a previously released offender. As a result, a preferred measurement of recidivism that is highlighted in this book is reinstitutionalization. Reinstitutionalism as a measurement of recidivism means that the ex-inmate had been rearrested, processed, reconvicted, and reincarcerated into prison, either because of a technical violation or because of committing a new offense, or both. Reinstitutionalization into prison is a more conservative and exhaustive way of measuring recidivism rate that entails that a previously incarcerated and released offender waned back into prison.

Fourth, this study was limited to the extent to which the author was able to identify relevant and appropriate evidence-based literature (Duwe, 2017) on the subject and the issues that directly or indirectly relate to the subject matter studied. As Ubah (2002) observes tendentiously, it is a truism that there is a large body of research literature on the general subject of offender rehabilitation. However, not all this literature is appropriately relevant and/or credible for this book. The literature utilized here was selected in part because of two major principles: (1) the studies must specifically deal with prison-based postsecondary educational rehabilitation program; and (2) the studies must meet certain criteria suggested by Gerber and Fritsch (1995) as highly appropriate in this kind of research. As a result, literatures the author deemed as not appropriately relevant for this book were excluded.

DIRECTION FOR FUTURE RESEARCH

As is evident above, a great number of meta-analysis empirical studies on offender rehabilitation programs were examined and analyzed in this book. In part or in whole, each one of them offers an opportunity for us to be aware and appreciate different evidence and perspectives with regards to the state of effectiveness or lack of it of prison-based correctional rehabilitation programs in reducing offender recidivism rate. Be that as it may, some number of weaknesses can be attributed to this approach of research, and striking and well-known potential bias among them is the tendency for them to show greater positive effect sizes than nonpublished ones for various reasons, including the selection processes associated with the development, submission, and review of literatures for journal publication (Nally et al., 2012; Rothstein et al., 2005). However, whether this possibility is true or not with the results of the meta-analysis studies examined in this book is not clear because the result of the findings of the unpublished studies included in the meta-analyses also indicate positive findings in the same direction as the published ones. Therefore, it is important that future studies on the subject investigate the issue more thoroughly and rigorously so that greater lessons can be gleaned and deeper insights gained on the matter.

Almost all the empirical studies on the subject reviewed in this book do not go beyond establishing statistical association in their analysis. However, among other things, this book calls on future researchers to go beyond establishing only statistical association when analyzing the impact(s) of correctional education on offender recidivism. They may do so by exploring the general question of what is it about correctional education programs that lead to the association with offender recidivism? In doing so, they should look out for the issue of spurious relationship ignored by just about all the studies on the subject reviewed here.

Different ways of measuring recidivism are identified and analyzed in this book. It seems that some of the measurements are seriously limited in their utility thereby making it difficult for them to offer a rigorous and conservative measurement of recidivism that is capable of accounting for all the layers that are supposed to be involved in the process. Some of the measurements at issue here include the use of rearrest and/or reconviction as indicators of recidivism. These indicators of recidivism are problematic especially when we are dealing with reincarceration. This is so because not all parolees who are arrested and/or convicted do return to prison. In that sense, a definition of recidivism should encompass "a return to prison." As a result, the measurement of recidivism highlighted and recommended in this book for future study is reinstitutionalization. Reinstitutionalism as a measure of recidivism means that the ex-inmate has been rearrested, reconvicted, and reincarcerated into the custody of a correctional center, either because of a technical violation or because of committing a new crime, or both (e.g., Duwe, 2017; Fogarty and Giles, 2018). Reinstitutionalization is a more conservative measure of recidivism and perhaps a more acceptable, credible, and sound way of measuring recidivism rate. The measure assures that a previously incarcerated and released offender waned back to prison.

In addition to the above suggestions made for future research on the subject, it is unfortunate that only a few studies have examined how the major changes in prison inmate college education funding (loss of Pell Grants) in 1994 affected the programs across penal institutions in the United States (for example, Batiuk, 1997; Tewksbury and Taylor, 1996; Tracy et al., 1998). It is even more unfortunate that, up to this moment, not much published research has attempted to determine how the profound major changes (loss of prison-based Pell Gants) in American corrections operations affected the recidivism rates of previously incarcerated and released offenders (Ubah, 2004). Similarly, rigorous studies should also be carried out on the impacts of the Second Chance Pell Pilot Initiative which began in 2016. As such, robust, systematic, and rigorous examination of these kinds of important external social changes on corrections and their consequences on offender recidivism across states and correctional agencies and institutions is needed now and in the future. An evaluation of these external environmental changes has, to a great degree, been ignored by researchers. The evaluation of these external changes is imperative because Pell Grants were the major sources of funding for postsecondary correctional education programs in the country. The evaluation would enable us to understand how recent developments or changes affected correctional education and offender recidivism rates across states and correctional agencies and institutions in the United States (Cantora et al., 2020; Mastrorilli, 2016; Ubah, 2005)

Thus, a renewed scholarly analysis of the effects of prison-based education on offender recidivism would enable us to determine whether correctional education "works" or "does not work." This analysis is important because research conducted to determine prison education's effects continues to produce mixed results and ongoing academic and political debates (for example, Anderson, 1981; Brown and Philo, 2017; Crow and Smykla, 2014; Davis et al., 2013; Duwe, 2017; Fain, 2019; Fox, 1950; Jenkins et al., 1995; Evans, 2019; Fogarty and Giles, 2018; Martinson, 1974; Matisoff, 1974; Porporino and Anderson, 1992; Sullivan, 1990; Ubah, 2001; Zink, 1962). A periodic determination of the effects of prison inmate college education programs on inmates after they are released to the larger community provides important measures that should not be ignored at all. But unfortunately, to a larger extent, they have been neglected in the past (Crow and Smykla, 2014; Latessa et al., 2015; Latessa, 1999; Ubah, 2004; Craig and Rogers, 1993).

Future investigations should focus on associate diploma and bachelor's degree programs rather than GED courses because of the following reasons: (a) the possible impact of 1994 Pell Grants elimination as well as the partial end of the elimination by the 2007 Second Chance Act and the 2015 Second Chance Pell Pilot Initiative concerned only postsecondary correctional programs; (b) participation in GED courses is mandatory in most states' correctional system; thus, there is no nonparticipating comparison group that would allow an estimate of education's impact on offenders; and (c) the assumption that if any prison-based education program will be a significant factor for reducing offender recidivism, college-level educational program is the most likely approach (Denney and Tynes, 2021; Duwe, 2017; Ubah, 2002). This is because the credentials that inmates acquire by participating in prison-based postsecondary education programs increase their legitimate human capital (resources that influence future activities in people, such as marketable legitimate skills, trades, network relationships) much more than GED programs do. These necessary human capital resources can help some inmates to "go straight" and abandon the life of crime when released to the larger society (e.g., Denney and Tynes, 2021; Bui and Morash, 2010; Bushway and Apel, 2013; Hershberger, 1987; Wang et al., 2010; Ellis and Lane, 1963).

As the debate over prison-based education continues to divide scholars, correctional practitioners, policy makers, and the public in general, this book adds to that debate by rigorously and critically examining different relevant issues. An example is the case of the usefulness or lack of it of prison-based education programs from the perspective of broader considerations of its other important values beyond merely its significant rate of recidivism reduction measure. As a result, the book instructs future studies on the subject to utilize multiple criteria in any determination of the usefulness or lack of it of the programs and with recidivism rate measurement alone.

It appears that three of the major examples of multiple issues stressed here for future study are intimately related. To capture this connection, future investigations on the subject should address: (1) the determination of the overall effects of correctional center's education programs on recidivism under Pell Grants; (2) the determination of the effects of correctional center's education on recidivism after the end of Pell Grants; and (3) the assessment of the effects of prison-based postsecondary education pilot sites of Second Chance Pell Pilot Initiatives.

Based on the literature, one would expect a reduction in recidivism as inmate access to correctional college education programs increase (i.e., during Pell Grants funding) and an increase in recidivism as inmate access to correctional college education program decreases (during no Pell Grants monies). The absence of such a reduction of recidivism in the first instance and absence of an increase of recidivism in the second instance would force the question of the validity of the idea that the elimination of financial aid for prison-based college education would have profound negative consequences for correctional postsecondary education programs on offender recidivism. If the two scenarios occur, then attention should be focused on the impact of "self-selection," i.e., of the overrepresentation, among education participants, of inmates already predisposed not to recidivate (e.g., Denney and Tynes, 2021; Fogarty and Giles, 2018; Drake and Fumia, 2017; Weisburd et al., 2017; Davis et al., 2013; Anderson, 1981; Meier and O'Toole, 2012; Ubah, 2001). This complex and critical social situation is among the major dilemmas that the Second Chance Pell Pilot Initiative is designed to ascertain and hopefully a good number of robust systematic studies would be able to do that because such knowledge and insights on this major development or social change, and similar others on corrections, are imperative for effective criminology, criminal justice, and public policy. It is therefore the hope of this author that, among other things, this study will help encourage in a serious way more interest on evidence-based approaches on prison-based college education programs policy, practice, reform, and evaluation research in the 21st century.

CONCLUSION AND QUALIFICATION

A number of conclusions can be drawn from this study. The first is that individual change perspectives of offender rehabilitation, such as moral development perspective, social-psychological development perspective, and opportunity perspective, are plausible ways of understanding, explaining, and predicting the rehabilitative potentials of correctional education programs, especially at the postsecondary levels. However, the perspectives are not without serious issues that need to be recognized and taken note of in any consideration of their usefulness. As a result, this book makes serious efforts to carry out a narrative of the strengths of the perspectives with a recognition of their weaknesses and, in the process, glean deeper insights and lessons. These are insights and lessons that might be too important and too costly to ignore in 21st century criminology, criminal justice, and public policy.

A critical narrative of the strengths and weaknesses of individual change perspectives (moral-development theory, social-psychological development theory, and opportunity theory) of offender rehabilitation as well as empirical literatures is carried out in this book because there has been a lack of adequate analysis of them in scholarly literature. The very few studies that have attempted to carry out such analysis have done so in passing without much serious attention given to the strengths and weaknesses of the perspectives and the empirical literatures. They seemed to stop precisely at a point where much more analysis of the strengths and weaknesses of the perspectives and empirical literature is needed. To fill the gap, a critical narrative of the strengths of the perspectives and the empirical literature with a recognition of their weaknesses is carried out.

Because theories are used both to explain and predict phenomena, offender habilitation theory is supposed to guide research, practice, and policy on offender rehabilitation. It should aid in part or in whole the explanation and/or prediction of the phenomenon of offender rehabilitation. It should be an explanation of how the process is supposed to work (e.g., Simon, 1993). It should ask the question of "how it works" which in turn leads to the determination of "what works and what doesn't in reducing recidivism" (e.g., Link and Williams, 2017; Crabtree at el., 2016; Latessa et al., 2015; Lin, 2000; Martinson, 1974). In effect, offender rehabilitation perspectives such as individual change approaches presented and analyzed in this book attempt to explain and/or predict prison-based education programs as mechanisms for offender rehabilitation and reintegration into the general society. Nevertheless, the approaches on their own might not account for the full truth of both why inmates exposed to such programs had a certain outcome and what exactly is possible with the programs as much as other forms of theoretical perspectives might. Ward and Maruna (2007:31) put it succinctly, "We accept that even our best theories may only be partially true and that it is possible that for any given scientific problem there could be more than one way of solving it."

Therefore, this book does not in any way claim to have answers for all the properties and elements of every theory of rehabilitation, nor does it pretend to account for all the truth of the phenomena under examination. Instead, it takes a closer look at some important individual change perspectives (moral-development theory, social-psychological development theory, and opportunity theory) on prison-based education rehabilitation programs and makes serious efforts to carry out a systematic narrative of their strengths and weaknesses for 21st century corrections research, policy, and practice.

The strengths-based premises of individual change perspectives articulated here form the arsenal from which proponents of correctional education programs draw their arguments for the continued provision, funding, and improvement of prison-based college education programs. On the other hand, the weaknesses of individual change perspectives pointed out here are part and parcel of the arsenal from which proponents of pessimistic persuasion of offender rehabilitation programs draw their arguments against prison-based correctional education programs (Ubah and Robinson, 2002; Ubah and Ubah, 2019). But all the technocratic language about the strengths and weaknesses of individual change perspectives of offender rehabilitation programs and their implications for corrections research, practice, and policy notwithstanding, it would be a serious mistake to use the evidence-based recidivism rate outcomes of offender rehabilitation programs as the sole indicator of prison-based rehabilitation program usefulness or lack of it, as Ubah (2014) and Denney and Tynes (2021) studies, for example, epitomized.

Assuming moral-development theory, social-psychological development theory, and opportunity theory has relevance for offender treatment, the theories are stated so cautiously as to raise the question of whether any available data could show any one of them to be preferable to others. Simply put, the idealistic theories can be described as speculative and not specific enough regarding the relationship between prison-based education programming and offender recidivism. Therefore, all the technocratic language of individual change perspectives of offender rehabilitation notwithstanding, the issues surrounding offender rehabilitation programs continue to divide scholars, policy makers, correctional practitioners, and the public at large. As Ubah (2002) demonstrated succinctly, literature on the subject is contradictory; some argue that, to a considerable extent, it accomplishes its purpose, whereas others think that it does not work. But current empirical evidence seems to suggest a much more positive result of the college-level programs than other programs (e.g., Bannin, 2021; Denney and Tynes, 2021; Duwe, 2017; Fogarty and Giles, 2018; Hall, 2015; Karpowitz, 2017; Pompoco et al., 2017).

It cannot be overemphasized that the assumptions of individual change perspectives of offender rehabilitation presented and analyzed here do not, in any way, hold the notion that the perspectives have all the answers of both why inmates exposed to rehabilitation programs had a certain outcome and what exactly is possible with the programs. Rather, the perspectives should be viewed as some of the plausible approaches with which we can explore the issue of offender rehabilitation. As such, more studies should continue to be conducted on the subject. But it will be most helpful that future studies try to recognize and appreciate the lessons and insights gleaned from this book. Such future studies can be imperative for criminology, criminal justice, and public policy because they can add more imagination and offer different perspectives in the discussion of the subject and, in the process, may provide deeper insights and critical lessons for corrections research, practice, and policy.

It can be concluded that the cumulative pessimistic efforts that eventually succeeded in the elimination of prison-based education Pell Grants in 1994 with the passage of the crime bill were much encouraged by the negative interpretations of Martinson's (1974) article by critics of correctional education programming. Martinson's "nothing works" verdict on correctional education is the most cited criminological literature on the subject. The question of whether Martinson was right or wrong in his conclusion that nothing works is not clearly and generally established by literature examined for this book. Yet, it seems clear that the pessimistic reaction of conservative politicians regarding prison-based offender rehabilitation did succeed in their political agenda in 1994 mainly because of the changes in the social fabric that triggered a corresponding shift in thinking and feeling about corrections—a thinking and feeling that are in tune with a climate of opinion increasingly frustrated with and hostile to a rehabilitative approach. However, most findings of empirical studies, especially the most recent ones found while examining literature for this project, lend support to the idea that participation in prison-based education programs especially at the postsecondary levels apparently serves to differentiate the more successful parolees from the unsuccessful ones. Nonetheless, it is important to note that currently there is evidence that the political climate on prison-based college offender rehabilitation and reintegration programs seem to be turning in favor of increased support for the programs (e.g., Denney and Tynes, 2021; Cantora et al., 2019; Fain, 2019; Mastrorilli, 2016).

It must be noted that the association between correctional attainment while in prison and the lives of formerly incarcerated persons when they return to the larger community is not satisfactorily captured by one simple measure of success or failure. For this reason, multiple criteria other than recidivism rates should be the right step in the right direction for future studies on the subject. What seems clear, however, is that prison-based postsecondary education is helpful to those inmates who are motivated to "go straight" by doing all it takes to turn their lives around and become law-abiding productive citizens. Yet, when all is said and done, the debate over prison-based education has not been resolved. Instead, it continues to divide scholars, policy makers, correctional practitioners, and the public at large.

Research literature suggests the abolition of Pell Grants for prison inmate college education continues to have a profound negative effect on most of the correctional education programs across the country (Cantora et al., 2019; Fain, 2019; United States Government Accountability Office, 2019; Muhlhausen and Hurwitz, 2019; Taylor and Tewksbury, 2002; Ubah, 2001; Petersilia, 2000). Thus, the elimination of the funding of the programs with federal monies in 1994 led to the continuing decrease of education programs in most correctional institutions across the United States. It also led to the loss of teachers who teach in the programs that were eliminated because of the cutback on prison inmate college education programs. What remains largely unclear is the impact of the elimination of Pell Grants for prison inmate college education on offender recidivism across the nation. The determination of a clear impact of the elimination of Pell Grants for inmate college education on offender recidivism across the nation is imperative for academic reasons as well as social and public policy. Whether the elimination of prison inmate college education Pell Grants for all eligible inmates in all institutions across the nation will continue to hold or will eventually reverse course in the future probably depends on what happens on the political arena, i.e., who comes to the seat of power at the national and/or state levels and what their belief systems, philosophies, and policies are on crime and corrections.

Most of the studies on the subject are mainly concerned with the debate over whether prison-based education works or does not work, while to a great degree, they ignore the need for an examination of academic, economic, political, policy, and social considerations of correctional education and offender recidivism (Ubah, 2014; Petersilia, 2001). The very few studies that have attempted to carry out such examination, have done so in passing without much attention to such considerations. They seemed to stop at a point where a more detailed examination of academic, economic, political, policy, and social considerations of correctional education and offender recidivism is needed. To fill this gap, an explicit examination of academic, political, policy, and social considerations of prison-based education and offender recidivism was carried out in this book. As can be seen, an examination of such considerations might be too important and too costly to ignore in 21st century criminology, criminal justice, and public policy.

It is important to keep in mind that as attractive as education programs might seem in their potential to positively affect prison-based institutional environments and offender recidivism rate, caution should be taken in having too much faith in the degree of impact they might have to positively affect, on their own, the offender recidivism rate. This is so because research has identified education as a moderate risk factor in predicating recidivism

(Denney and Tynes, 2021; Duwe, 2018). On the other hand, risk factors such as criminal history, antisocial personality pattern, criminal thinking, and antisocial peers have been identified as major risk factors for recidivism. These four major risk factors have been described as the "big four" recidivism risk factors (Duwe, 2018). In other words, the four risk factors are much more reliable in predicting recidivism than education. Duwe (2018:4) underscores this point by asserting that:

> Given that education and employment are moderate recidivism risk factors, it may be unreasonable to expect these programs to produce large reduction in recidivism. Moreover, even though education and employment interventions each address a criminogenic need (or recidivism risk factor), offenders often have multiple areas of need that contribute to their recidivism risk.

In addition to all of these interacting factors of recidivism, the environments offenders return to can be major factors of recidivism as well (e.g., Veysey, 2008).

With all due considerations and qualifications, it is important to note that the arguments and conclusions made in this book do not, in any way, hold the illusion that all the ills of crime and criminals would be eradicated with correctional education programs alone. Rather, they should be understood and considered as some of the viable options in our tool kit through which we can make some difference in our attempts to address some of the issues and problems of crime and our penal systems well into the 21st century.

References

Afrifor, C. A., Atere, A. A., and Nuoghalu, C. O. 2012. Gender differences, trend, and pattern recidivism among inmates in selected Nigerian prisons. *European Scientific Journal* 8(24):25–44.

Agnew, R. 2001. Building on the foundation of general strain theory: Specifying the types of strain most likely to lead to crime and delinquency. *Journal of Research in Crime & Delinquency* 38:319–61.

Agresti, A., and Finlay, B. 1997. *Statistical Methods for the Social Sciences*. 3rd ed. San Francisco: Dellen.

Alarid, L. F., and del Carmen, R. V. 2001. *Community-based Corrections*. 8th ed. Belmont, CA: Wadsworth/Cengage Learning.

Aldrich, H. E., and Pfeffer, J. 1976. Environments of organization. *Annual Review of Sociology* 2:79–105.

Anderson, C. D. 1999. "The Mystery of the Falling Crime Rate." In *Criminal Justice*, 22nd ed., Annual Editions, edited by J. L. Victor, 29–33.

Anderson, D. B. 1981. The relationship between correctional education and parole success. *Journal of Offender Counseling, Services & Rehabilitation* 5:13–25.

Anderson, D. B., Schumacker, R. E., and Anderson, S. L. 1991. Release characteristics and parole success. *Journal of Offender Rehabilitation* 17:133–45.

Andrews, D. A., and Bonta, J. 2003. *The Psychology of Criminal Conduct*. 3rd ed. Cincinnati, OH: Anderson.

Andrews, D. A., Bonta, J., and Wormith, S. J. 2006. The recent past and near future of risk and need assessment. *Crime & Delinquency* 52:7–27.

Antonowicz, D. H. 2005. "The Reasoning and Rehabilitation Program: Outcome Evaluations with Offenders." In *Social Problem Solving and Offending: Evidence, Evaluation, and Evolution*, edited by M. McMurran and J. McGuire. Chichester, UK: John Wiley.

Arbuthnot, J., and Gordon, D. A. 1986. Behavioral and cognitive effects of a moral reasoning development intervention for high-risk behavior-disordered adolescents. *Journal of Consulting & Clinical Psychology* 54:208–18.

Austin, J. 2017. Limits of prison education. *Criminology & Public Policy* 16:563–69.

Austin, J., and Irwin, J. 2001. *It Is About Time: American's Imprisonment Binge*. 3rd ed. Belmont, CA: Wadsworth.

Austin, M. C. 1987. Inmate education: A wise use of correctional funds. *Corrections Today* (August).

Bailey, W. C. 1966. Correctional outcome: An evaluation of 100 reports. *Journal of Criminal Law, Criminology & Police Science* 57:153–60.

Bandura, A. 1979. "The Social Learning Perspective: Mechanisms of Aggression." In *Psychology of Crime and Criminal Justice*, edited by H. Toch. New York: Holt, Rinehart & Winston.

Barth, R. P., Guo, S., and McCrae, J. S. 2010. Propensity Score Matching in Criminology and Criminal Justice. In *The Handbook of Quantitative Criminology*, edited by A. R. Piquero and D. Weisburd. New York: Springer.

Barkan, S. E. 2018. *Criminology: A Sociological Understanding*. 7th ed. New York: Pearson.

Bartol, C. R. 1995. *Criminal Behavior: A Psychological Approach*. 4th ed. Englewood Cliffs, NJ: Prentice Hall.

Basic, J. 2021. The unexamined life is not worth living. *Curious*:1–10.

Bastedo, M. N. 2004. "Open systems theory. The Sage Encyclopedia of Education Leadership and Administration.

Batiuk, M. 1997. The state of post-secondary correctional education in Ohio. *Journal of Correctional Education* 48:70–73.

Batiuk, M., Lahm, K., McKeever, M., Wilcox, N., and Wilcox, P. 2005. Disentangling the effects of correctional education: Are current policies misguided? An event history analysis. *Criminal Justice* 5(1):55–74.

Bays, B. 1999. Habitat at Taylorville: One example of how prisons can successfully partner with outside agencies for restorative justice. *Journal of Correctional Education* 50:48–50.

Becker, G. S. 1964. *Human Capital: A Theoretical and Empirical Analysis, with Special Reference to Education*. New York: National Bureau of Economic Research.

Berghuis, M. 2018. Reentry programs for adult male offender recidivism and reintegration: A systematic review and meta-analysis. *International Journal of Offender Therapy & Comparative Criminology* 62(14):4655–76.

Bernard, T. J. 1990. Angry aggression among the truly disadvantaged. *Criminology* 28:73–96.

Blackburn, F. S. 1981. Relationships between recidivism and participation in a community college program for incarcerated offenders. *Journal Correctional Education* 32:23–25.

Blevins, K. R. 2017. "Positivism." In *The Routledge Companion to Criminological Theory and Concepts*, edited by A. Brisman, E. Carrabine, and N. South. New York: Routledge.

Blumer, H. 1969. *Symbolic Interactionism: Perspective and Method*. Englewood Cliffs, NJ: Prentice Hall.

Bohm, R. M., and Haley, K. N. 2002. *Introduction to Criminal Justice*. 3rd ed. Peoria, Illinois: Glencoe McGraw Hill.

Bohrnstedt, G. W., and Knoke, D. 1994. *Statistical for Social Data Analysis*. 3rd ed. Itasca, Illinois: F. E. Peacock.

Braithwaite, J., and Strang, H. 2001. "Introduction: Restorative Justice and Civil Society." In *Restorative Justice and Civil Society*, pp.1–13. New York: Cambridge University Press.

Brazell, D., Crayton, A., Mukamai, D., Solomon, A., and Lindahl, N. 2009. "From the Classroom to the Community: Exploring the Role of Education during Incarceration and Reentry." Urban Institute Justice Policy Center, 1–50.

Brennan, T. 2012. Signaling and meta-analytic evaluations in the presence of latent offender groups: The importance of coherent target group specification. *Criminology & Public Policy* 11(1):61–72.

Brewster, L. 2010. The California arts-in-corrections music programme: A quantitative study. *International Journal of Community Music* 3(1):33–46.

Brown, J. C., and Philo, R. L. 2017. *The Corr of the American Criminal Justice System: Lessons and the Anatomy of an American Tragedy*. Dubuque, IA: Kendall Hunt.

Bui, H. N., and Morash, M. 2010. The impact of network relationships, prison experiences, and internal transformation on women's success after prison release. *Journal of Offender Rehabilitation* 40:1–22.

Burke, L. O., and Vivian, J. E. 2001. The effect of college programing on recidivism rates at the Hampden County House of Correction: A 5-year study. *Journal of Correctional Education* 52:160–62.

Burton, V. S., Dunaway, R. G., and Kopache, R., 1993. Research Note: To punish or rehabilitate? A research note assessing the purposes of state correctional departments as defined by state legal codes. *Journal of Crime & Justice* XVI 1:177–88.

Bushway, S. D., and Apel, R. 2012. A signaling perspective on employment-based reentry programming: Training completion as a desistance signal. *Criminology & Public Policy* 11:21–50.

Cantora, A., Miller, J., and White, K. 2019. Implementing Pell: Challenges and successes of implementing the U.S. Department of Education's Second Chance Pell experimental sites initiative. *Journal of Correctional Education* 71(1):2–17.

Caudy, M. S., Taxman, F. S., Tang, L. L., and Watson, C. 2016. "Evidence Mapping to Advance Justice Practice." In *What Works in Crime and Rehabilitation: Lessons from Systematic Reviews*, edited by D. Weisburd, D. P. Farrington, and C. Gills. New York: Springer.

Center on Crime, Community and Culture. 1997. "Education as Crime Prevention: Providing Education to Prisoners." Research Brief Occupational Paper Series (September) 2:1–13.

Chappell, C. 2004. Post-secondary correctional education and recidivism: A meta-analysis of research conducted 1990–1999. *Journal of Correctional Education* 55(2): 148–69.

Clark, K. J., Mitchell, M. M., Fahmy, C., Pyrooz, D. C., and Decker, S. H. 2020. What if they are all high risk for attrition? Correlates of retention in a longitudinal study of reentry from prison. *International Journal of Offender Therapy & Comparative Criminology* (November 5):1–40.

Clear, T. R. 2007. *Imprisoning Communities: How Mass Incarceration Makes Disadvantaged Neighborhoods Worse*. New York: Oxford University.

Clear, T. R., and Cole, G. F. 2003. *American Corrections*. 6th ed. Belmont, CA: Thomson/Wadsworth.

Clear, T. R., Cole, G. F., and Reisig, M. D. 2013. *American Corrections*. 10th ed. Belmont, CA: Thomson/Wadsworth.

Clear, T. R., and Karp, D. R. 1999. *The Community Justice Ideal*. Boulder, CO: Westview Press.

Clemmer, D. 1958. *The Prison Community*. New York: Holt, Rinehart & Winston.

Cloward, R. A., and Ohlin, L. E. 1960. *Delinquency and Opportunity*. New York: Free Press of Glencoe.

Cochran, A. W. 1965. Is education of value to the parolee? *Journal of Correctional Education* (April) 17:22–24.

Colvin, G. 1916. *Humans Are Underrated: What High Achievers Know That Brilliant Machines Never Will*. New York: Portfolio/Penguin.

Colvin, M. 1992. *The Penitentiary in Crisis: From Accommodation to Riot in New Mexico*. New York: State University of New York Press.

Contardo, J., and Tolbert, M. 2008. *Prison Postsecondary Education: Bridging Learning from Incarceration to the Community*. Washington, DC: Urban Institute.

Crabtree, J. L., Ohm, D., Wall, J. M., and Ray, J. 2016. Evaluation of a prison occupational therapy informal education program: A pilot study. *Occupational Therapy International Journal* 43:401–11.

Craig, D., and Rogers, R. 1993. Vocational training in prison: A case study of maximum feasible misunderstanding. *Journal of Offender Rehabilitation* 20:1–20.

"The Crime of Prison Illiteracy." 1996. *Chicago Tribune*, March 25, p.10.

Cronbach, L. 1982. "Prudent Aspirations for Social Inquiry." In *The Social Sciences: The Nature and Uses*, edited by W. H. Kruskal. Chicago: University of Chicago Press.

Crow, M. S., and Smykla, J. O. 2014. *Offender Reentry: Rethinking Criminology and Criminal Justice*. Burlington, MA: Jones & Bartlett Learning.

Cullen, F. T. 2013. "Rehabilitation: Beyond Nothing Works." In *Crime and Justice: A Review of Research*, vol. 42, edited by M. Tonry. Chicago: University of Chicago Press.

___________. 2007. Making rehabilitation corrections' guiding paradigm. *Criminology & Public Policy* 6:717–27.

___________. 2005. The twelve people who saved rehabilitation: How the science of criminology made a difference. *Criminology* 43(1):1–42.

Cullen, F. T., and Gendreau, P. 1989. "The Effectiveness of Corrections Rehabilitation." In *The American Prisons: Issues in Research and Policy*, edited by L. Goldstein and D. L. MacKenzie, pp. 23–44.

Cullen, F. T., Jonson, C. L., and Nagin, D. S. 2011. Prisons do not reduce recidivism: The high cost of ignoring science. *Prison Journal* 91:48–65.

Curren, D., and Renzetti, C. 1996. *Social Problems: Society in Crisis*. 4th ed. Boston: Allyn & Bacon.

Davidson, H. S. 1997. Political processes in prison education: A history. *Journal of Correctional Education* 48(3):136–41.

Davis, L. M., Bozick, R., Steele, J. L., and Saunders, J.N.V. 2013. *Evaluating the Effectiveness of Correctional Education*. Washington, DC: RAND Corporation.

Delisi, M., and Conis, P. J. 2019. *American Corrections: Theory, Policy, and Practice*. 3rd ed. Burlington, MA: Jones & Bartlett Learning.

Denney, M.G.T., and Tynes, R. 2021. The effects of college in prison and policy implications. *Justice Quarterly* 38(7): 1542–66.

Department of Corrections. 2019. "Second Chance Pell extended through 2019–2020." Department of Corrections (March 12).

Dilulio, J., Jr. 1987. *Governing Prisons: A Comparative Study of Correctional Management*. New York: Free Press/Macmillan.

Dominguez, P., and Raphael, S. 2015. The role of the cost-of-crime literature in bridging the gap between social science research and policy making potentials and limitations. *Criminology & Public Policy* 14:589–632.

Dowden, C., and Andrews, D. A. 2003. Does family intervention work for delinquents? Results of a meta-analysis. *Canadian Journal of Criminology & Criminal Justice* 42:449–67.

___________. 2000. Effective correctional treatment and violent reoffending: A meta-analysis. *Canadian Journal of Criminology & Criminal Justice* 42:449–67.

___________. 1999a. What works in young offenders: A meta-analysis. *Forum on Corrections Research* 11:21–24.

Drake, E. K., and Fumia, D. 2017. Evolution of correctional education evaluation and directions for future research. *Criminology & Public Policy* 16:549–61.

Duguid, S. 1992. Becoming interested in other things: The impact of education in prison. *Journal of Correctional Education* (March) 17:38–43.

___________. 1981. Prison education and criminal choice: The context of decision–making. *Canadian Journal of Criminology* 23:421–38.

Durose, M. R., Cooper, A. D., and Snyder, H. N. 2014. *Recidivism of Prisoners Released in 30 States in 2005: Patterns from 2005 to 2010*. Washington, DC: Bureau of Justice Statistics.

Duwe, G. 2018. *The Effectiveness of Education and Employment Programming for Prisoners*. American Enterprise Institute, 1–12.

___________. 2017a. *Rethinking Prison: A Strategy for Evidence-Based Reform*. American Enterprise Institute, 1–36.

___________. 2017b. *The Use and Impact of Correctional Programming for Inmates Pre- and Post-Release Outcomes*. National Institute of Justice, 1–39.

Duwe, G., and Clark, V. 2017a. Nothing will work unless you did: The predicators of post-prison employment. *Criminal Justice & Behavior* 44:657–77.

___________. 2017b. The rehabilitative ideal versus the criminogenic reality: The consequences of warehousing prisoners. *Corrections, Policy, Practice & Research* 2:41–69.

Duwe, G., Hallett, M., Hays, J., Jang, S. J., and Johnson, B. R. 2015. Bible college participation and prison misconduct: A preliminary analysis. *Journal of Offender Rehabilitation* 54:371–90.

Ebaugh, H.R.F. 1988. *Becoming an Ex: The Process of Role Exit*. Chicago: University of Chicago Press.

Edwards, K. L. 2014. "Prison work: Transforming Identity and Reducing Recidivism." In *Offender Reentry: Rethinking Criminology and Criminal Justice*, edited by M. S. Crow and J. O. Smykla, pp. 51–71. Burlington, MA: Jones & Bartlett.

Eichenthal, D. R., and Blatchford, L. 2001. "Prison Crime in New York State." Annual Editions Corrections, pp. 62–66.

Elechi, O. O. 1999. Victims under restorative justice systems: The Afikpo (Ehugbo) Nigeria model. *International Review of Victimology* 6:359–75.

Ellis, R. A., and Lane, W. C. 1963. Structural support for upward mobility. *American Sociological Review* 28:743–56.

Emery, L. 2020. Nonprofit provides pathway from prison through higher education. The Examiner News.com, 1–6.

Erisman, W., and Contardo, J. 2005. *Learning to Reduce Recidivism: A 50-State Analysis of Post-Secondary Correctional Education Policy*. Washington, DC: Institute for Higher Education Policy.

Evans, D. 2018. The elevating connection of higher education in prison: An incarcerated student's perspective. *Critical Education* 9(11):1–14.

Fabiano, E. A. 1991. How education can be correctional and how corrections can be educational. *Journal of Correctional Education* 42:100–106.

Fain, P. 2019. Report on state of postsecondary education in prison. *Inside Higher Ed* (June) 3:1–4.

Farkas, G. M. 1987. New partnership: Industries and education/training benefits institutions and inmates. *Corrections Today* (February):52–54.

Farrington, K. 1992. The modern prison as total institution? Public perception versus objective reality. *Crime & Delinquency* 38:6–26.

Fogarty, J., and Giles, M. 2018. "Recidivism and Education Revisited: Evidence for the USA." Working Paper 1806. Agricultural and Resource Economics, University of Western Australia, Crawley, Australia.

Fox, V. 1950. Michigan's experiment in minimum security penology. *Journal of Criminal Law, Criminology & Police Science* 2:150–66.

French, S. A., and Gendreau, P. 2006. Reducing prison misconducts: What works? *Criminal Justice & Behavior* 33:185–218.

Gaes, G. G. 2008. "The Impact of Prison Education Programs on Post-Release Outcomes." Reentry Roundtable on Education, 1–31.

Garfinkel, H. 1956. Conditions of successful degradation ceremonies. *American Journal of Sociology* 61:420–24.

Gehring, T. 1997. Post-secondary education for inmates: An history inquiry. *Journal of Correctional Education* 48:46–55.

Gendreau, P. 1996. Offender rehabilitation: What we know and what needs to be done. *Criminal Justice & Behavior* 23:144–61.

Gendreau, P., and Ross, R. R. 1979. Effective correctional treatment: Bibliotherapy for cynics. *Crime & Delinquency* 25:463–89.

Gerber, J., and Fritsch, E. 1995. Adult academic and vocational correctional education programs: A review of recent research. *Journal of Offender Rehabilitation* 22:119–42.

Ginsberg, R. 2014. Knowing that we are making a difference: A case for critical prison programming. *Studies in Law, Politics, and Society*, special issue: *The Beautiful Prison*, 33–47.

Glaser, D. 1975. Achieving better questions: A half century's progress in correctional research. *Federal Probation*, pp. 3–9.

Goffman, E. 1961. *Asylums: Essay on the Social Situation Mental, Patients and Other Inmates*. Garden City, NY: Anchor.

Gordon, H., and Weldon, B. 2003. The impact of career and technical education programs on adult offenders: Learning behind bars. *Journal of Correctional Education* 54(4):200–209.

Goredki, J. 1979. *A Theory of Criminal Justice*. New York: Columbia University Press.

Gunn, P. 1999. Learner and instructor need in a correctional setting. *Journal of Correctional Education* 50:74–82.

Hackman, K. M. 1997. Correctional education: Challenges and changes. *Journal of Correctional Education* 48:74–78.

Hall, L. L. 2015. Correctional education and recidivism: Toward a tool for reduction. *Journal of Correctional Education* 66(2):4–28.

Halstead, S. 1999. Educational discipline using the principles of restorative justice. *Journal of Correctional Education* 50(2):42–47.

Hanson, R., Gordon, A., Harris, A., Marques, J., Murphy, W., Quinsey, V., and Seto, M. 2002. First report of the collaborative outcome data project on the effectiveness of psychological treatment for sex offenders. *Sexual Abuse: Journal of Research & Treatment* 14:167–94.

Hawkins, D. F. 1995. *Ethnicity, Race, and Crime: Perspectives Across Time and Place*. Albany, NY: State University of New York Press.

Hedges, L. V., Tipton, E., and Johnson, M. C. 2010. Robust variance estimation in meta-regression with dependent effect size estimates. *Research Synthesis Method* 1(1):39–65.

Herrschaft, B. A., Veysey, B. M., Tuman-Carbone, H. R., and Christian, J. 2009. Gender differences in the transformation narrative: Implications for revised reentry strategies for female offenders. *Journal of Offender Rehabilitation* 48(6):463–82.

Hershberger, S. L. 1987. Vocational education preparing for life outside. *Corrections Today* (August): 128–32.

Hickert, A., Bushway, S., Nieuwbeerta, P., and Dirkzwager, A. 2021. Confinement as a two-stage turning point: Do changes in identity or social structure predict subsequent changes in criminal activity. *Criminology*:71–107.

Hipp, J. R., Petersilia, J., and Turner, S. 2010. Parolee recidivism in California: The effect of neighborhood context and social service agency characteristics. *Criminology* 48(4): 947–79.

Hirschi, T. 1969. *Causes of Delinquency*. Berkeley: University of California Press.

Hobler, B. 1999. Correctional education: Now and in the future. *Journal of Correctional Education* 50:102–5.

Holloway, J., and Moke, P. 1986. "Post-Secondary Correctional Education: An Evaluation of Parolees Performance." Research/technical report (May), pp. 143.

Hull, K., Forrester, S., Brown, J., Jobe, D., and McCullen, C. 2000. Analysis of recidivism rates for participants of the academic/vocational/transition education programs offered by the Virginia Department of Correctional Education. *Journal of Correctional Education* 51(2):256–61.

Hunt, K. S., and Dumville, R. 2016. "Recidivism among Federal Prisoners: A Comprehensive Overview." United States Sentencing Commission.

Igbo, E. U. M, and Ugwuoke, C. U. 2003. Recidivism in Enugu prison. *Nigerian Journal of Research & Production* 3(3):26–35.

Illinois Criminal Justice Information Authority. 1991. Trends and Issues 91: "Education and Criminal Justice in Illinois."

Inciardi, J. A. 1987. *Criminal Justice*. 2nd ed. San Diego, CA: Harcourt Brace Jovanovich.

Ioannidis, J.P.A., Stanley, T. D., and Doucouliagos, H. 2017. The power of bias in economics research. *Economic Journal* 127(605): F236–F265.

Irwin, J. 1985. *The Jail: Managing the Underclass in American Society*. Berkeley: University of California Press.

___________. 1970. *The Felon*. Englewood Cliffs, NJ: Prentice Hall.

Irwin, J., and Austin, J. 1997. *It Is About Time: American's Imprisonment Binge*. Belmont, CA: Wadsworth.

Jablecki, L. T. 2000. Prison inmates meet Socrates. http://www.article.findarticle.-com/p/article/mi_m1374/is_3_60/a i_62111876/print.

Jacobs, J. B. 1977. *Stateville: The Penitentiary in Mass Society*. Chicago: University of Chicago Press.

Jacobs, J. B., McGahey, R., and Minion, R. 1984. Ex-offender employment, recidivism, and manpower policy: CETA, TJTC, and future initiatives. *Crime & Delinquency* 30:486–506.

Jancic, M. 1998. Does correctional education have an effect on recidivism? *Journal of Correctional Education* 49:152–61.

Jenkins, D. H., Steurer, S. J., and Pendry, J. 1995. A post release follow-up of correctional education program completers released in 1990–1991. *Journal of Correctional Education* 46:20–23.

Johnson, E. H. 1964. *Crime, Corrections, and Society*. Homewood, Il: Dorsey Press.

Johnson, R. 2002. *Hard Time: Understanding and Reforming the Prison*. Stamford, CT: Thomson.

Karpowitz, D. 2017. *College in Prison: Reading in an Age of Mass Incarceration*. New Brunswick, NJ: Rutgers University Press.

Karstedt, S. 2008. In search of the tipping point. *The Criminologist* (March/April) 33(2): 3–5.

Kelly, F. J., Beggs, D. L., McNeil, K. A., Eichelberger, T., and Lyon, J. 1969. *Research Design in the Behavioral Sciences: Multiple Regression Approach*. London: Feffer & Simon.

Kirk, D. S. 2012. Residential change as a turning point in the life course of crime: Desistance of temporary cessation? *Criminology* 50(2):329–58.

Krisberg, B. A., Marchionna, S., and Hartney, C. J. 2019. *American Corrections: Concepts and Controversies*. 2nd ed. Los Angeles: Sage.

Kubrin, C. E., and Stewart, E. A. 2006. Predicting who reoffends: The neglected role of neighborhood context in recidivism studies. *Criminology* 44:165–97.

Kurlychek, M., Bushway, S. D., and Brame, R. 2012. Long-term crime desistance and recidivism patterns: Evidence from the Essex County convicted felon study. *Criminology* 50:71–104.

Lahm, K. F. 2009. Educational participation and inmate misconduct. *Journal of Offender Rehabilitation* 41:196–204.

Langenbach, M., North, M. Y., Aagard L., and Chown, W. 1990. Televised instruction in Oklahoma prison: A study of recidivism and disciplinary action. *Journal of Correctional Education* 41:87–85.

Latessa, E. 2012. Why work is important, and how to improve the effectiveness of correctional reentry programs that target employment. *Criminology & Public Policy* 11(1): 87–92.

____________. 1999. Classifying and assessing offenders: Understanding the criminal mind. *Corrections* 2:8.

Latessa, E., Listwan, S. J, and Koetzle, D. 2015. *What Works (and Doesn't) in Reducing Recidivism*. London: Routledge.

Lattimore, P. K., Steffey, D. M, and Visher, C. A. 2010. Prisoner reentry in the first decade of the twenty-first century. *Victims & Offenders* 5:253–67.

Lilly, J. R., Cullen, F. T., and Ball, R. A. 2010. *Criminological Theory: Context and Consequences*. Thousand Oaks, CA: Sage.

Lejins, P. P. 1971. *Sourcebook on Prison Education: Past, Present, and Future*. Springfield, IL: Charles C. Thomas.

Lewen, J. 2014. Prison higher education and social transformation. *Saint Louis University Public Law Review* 33:353–62.

Lipton, D., Martinson, R., and Wilks, J. 1975. *The Effectiveness of Correctional Treatment*. New York: Praeger.

Littlefield, J. F., and Wolford, B. I. 1982. Survey of higher education in United States correctional institutions. *Journal of Correctional Education* 33(1):14–18.

Lin, A. C. 2000. *Reform in the Making: The Implementation of Social Policy in Prison*. Princeton, NJ: Princeton University Press.

Linden, S.V.D. 2015. Green prison programmes, recidivism, and mental health: A primer. *Criminal Behaviour & Mental Health* 25:338–42.

Linden, R., and Perry, L. 1982. The effectiveness of prison education programs. *Journal of Offender Counseling, Services & Rehabilitation* 6:43–57.

Link, A. J., and Williams, D. J. 2017. Leisure functioning and offender rehabilitation: A Correctional exploration into factors affecting successful reentry. *International Journal of Offender Therapy & Comparative Criminology* 61(2):150–70.

Lipsey, M. W., and Cullen, F. T. 2007. The effectiveness of correctional rehabilitation: A review of systematic review. *Annual Review of Law and Social Science* 3:297–320.

Lockwood, D. 1991. "Prison Higher Education and Recidivism: A Program Evaluation." In *The Year Book of Correctional Education*, pp.187–201.

Losel, F. 1998. "Effective Correctional Programming: What Empirical Research Tells Us and What It Doesn't." In *Incarcerating Criminals: Prisons and Jails in Social and Organizational Context*, edited by T. J. Flanagan, J. W. Marquart, and K. G. Adams, pp. 20–214. Oxford, UK: Oxford University Press.

Mackenzie, D. L. 2006. *What Works in Corrections? Reducing the Criminal Activities of Offenders and Delinquents*. Cambridge, UK: Cambridge Press.

Mallender, J., and Tierney, R. 2016. "Economic Analysis." In *What Works in Crime and Rehabilitation: Lessons from Systematic Reviews*, edited by D. Weisburd, D. P. Farrington, and C. Gills. New York: Springer.

Mandel, N. G. 1963. "Crime Revisited." Minnesota Department of Corrections.

Marlowe, D. B. 2006. When "what works" never did: Dodging the "Scarlet M" in correctional rehabilitation. *Criminology & Public Policy* 5:339–47.

Martin, G. 2016. Six ways President Obama reformed America's criminal justice system. *NewsOne* (November) 15:1–8.

Martinson, R. 1979. New findings, new view: A note of caution regarding sentencing and reform. *Hofstra Law Review* 7:243–58.

___________. 1976. California research at the crossroads. *Crime & Delinquency* 22:180–91.

___________. 1974. What works? Questions and answers about prison reform. *The Public Interest* (Spring) 35: 22–55.

Maruna, S. 2012. Elements of successful desistance signaling. *Criminology & Public Policy* 11(1): 73–86.

___________. 2001. *Making Good: How Ex-Convicts Reform and Rebuild Their Lives.* Washington, DC: American Psychological Association.

Maruna, S., and LeBel, T. 2003. Welcome home? Examining the reentry court concept from a strengths-based perspective. *Western Criminology Review* 4(2): 91–107.

Mastrorilli, M. E. 2016. With Pell Grants rising: A review of the contemporary empirical literature on prison postsecondary education. *Journal of Correctional Education* 67(2): 44–60.

Matisoff, D, 1973. "A Study of the Effect of Correctional Education on Recidivism at a Selected Minimum Security Correctional Center." Unpublished dissertation, Southern Illinois University, Carbondale.

Matsuyama, K, and Prell, L. (2010). Education, employment, and offender reentry. *Correction Today* 72 (4): 90–91.

McAdams, D. P. 1994. "Can Personality Change? Levels of Stability and Growth in Personality across the Life Span." In *Can Personality Change?*, edited by T. F. Heatherton and J. L. Weinberger. Washington, DC: American Psychological Association.

McCarthy, B. R., McCarthy, B. J., and Leone, M. C. 2001. *Community-Based Corrections*. 4th ed. Belmont, CA: Wadsworth/Thomson Learning.

McKean, J., and Byers, B. 2000. *Data Analysis for Criminal Justice and Criminology: Practice and Applications*. Boston: Allyn & Bacon.

McKelvey, B. 1977. *American Prisons: A History of Good Intentions*. Glen Ridge, NJ: Patterson Smith.

McMahon, M. W. 1992. *The Persistent Prison? Rethinking Decarceration and Penal Reform*. Toronto, Canada: University of Toronto Press.

Mead, G. H. 1934. *Mind, Self, and Society: From the Standpoint of a Social Behaviorist*. Chicago: University of Chicago Press.

Mears, D. P., and Mestre, J. 2012. Prisoner reentry, employment, signaling, and the better identification of desisters: Introduction to the special issue. *Criminology & Public Policy* 11(1):5–16.

Mears, D. P., Cochran, J.A.C., and Bhati, A S. 2016. Recidivism and time served in prison. *Journal of Criminal Law & Criminology* 106(1):83–124.

Meier, K. J., and O'Toole, L. J., Jr. 2012. Subjective organizational performance and measurement error: Common source bias and spurious relationships. *Journal of Public Administration Research & Theory*, pp. 1–28.

Meiser, R. F. 1989. *Crime and Society*. Boston: Allyn & Bacon.

Merton, R. 1938. Social structure and anomie. *American Sociological Review* 3:672–82.

Messner, S. F., and Rosenfeld, R. 2013. *Crime and the American Dream*. 5th ed. Belmont: CA: Cengage Learning.

Miethe, T. D., and McCorkle, R. 1998. *Crime Profile: The Anatomy of Dangerous Persons, Places, and Situation*. Los Angeles: Roxbury Publishing.

Miller, J. G. 1997. *Search and Destroy: African-American Males in the Criminal Justice System*. Cambridge, UK: Cambridge University Press.

Miller, R. J. 2012. "Devolving the Carceral State." Paper presented at the American Society of Criminology, Chicago, Illinois, November.

Monroe, W. E., and Whitson, C. M. 1975. Unique prison school district emphasizes vocational education training. *School Shop* 34:38–40.

Morenoff, J. D., and Harding, D. J. 2014. Incarceration, prisoner reentry, and communities. *Annual Review Social* (July) 40:411–29.

Morphonios, E., and Wilson, M. 1991. *Maximum Morphonios: The Life and Times of America's Toughest Judge*. New York: William Morrow.

Morris, C. W. 1962. *Mind, Self, and Society: From the Standpoint of Social Behaviorist*. Chicago: University of Chicago Press.

Muhlhausen, D. B., and Hurwitz, H. J. 2019. "First Step-Act: Best Practices for Academic and Vocational Education for Offenders." National Institute of Justice, U.S. Department of Justice.

Muraskin, R. 2010. Introduction to "Prisoner Reentry: The Iron Law of Imprisonment." In *Key Correctional Issues*, 2nd ed., edited by R. Muraskin, pp. 79–91. Upper Saddle River, NJ: Prentice Hall.

Mutchnick, R. J., and Lewis, J. A. 2017. *Criminology*. Dubuque, IA: Kendall Hunt.

Nally, J., Lockwood, S., Knutson, K., and Ho, T. 2012. An evaluation of the effect of correctional education program on post-release recidivism and employment: An empirical study in Indiana. *Journal of Correctional Education* 63(1):69–89.

National Humanities Medal. 2015. Prison university project. National Endowment for the Humanities: 1–4.

Ness, D. V., and Strong, K. H. 1997. *Restoring Justice*. Cincinnati, OH.

Nicholas, B. 1996. Clinton makes future his centerpiece. *USA Today* (June 5).

Norusis, M. J. 1990. *The SPSS Guide to Data Analysis*. Chicago IL:

Odling-Smee, F. J., Laland, K. N., and Feldman, M. W. 2003. *Niche Construction: The Neglected Process in Evolution*. Princeton, NJ: Princeton University Press.

Ogloff, J. R. O., and Davis, M. R. 2004. Advances in offender assessment and rehabilitation: Contributions of the risk-need-responsivity approach. *Psychology, Crime & Law* 10:229–42.

O'Neil, M. 1990. Correctional higher education: Reduced recidivism? *Journal of Correctional Education* 41:28–31.

Orpinas, P., Kelder, S., Murray, N., Fourney, N., Conroy, J., McReynolds, L., and Peter, R., Jr. 1996. Critical issues in implementing a comprehensive violence prevention program for middle schools: Translating theory into practice. *Education & Urban Society* 28:456–72.

Osborne, M. 2019. "Evaluation of North Carolina's Prison-Based Postsecondary Education Program Offers Important Insights." Carolina Center for Public Policy Research, pp. 1–8.

Palmer, S. M. 2012. Postsecondary correctional education: Recognizing and overcoming barriers to success. *Adult Learning* 23:163–69.

Palmer, T. 1975. Martinson revisited. *Journal of Research in Crime & Delinquency* (July):133–52.

Paparozzi, M., and Guy, R. 2014. "Reentry: Parole by Any Other Name." In *Offender Reentry: Rethinking Criminology and Criminal Justice*, edited by M. S. Crow and J. O. Smyka, pp. 7–20. Burlington, MA: Jones & Bartlett.

Parsons, T. 1968. *The Structure of Social Action*. New York: Free Press/Macmillan

Parsons, T., and Gidden, A. 1976. *Max Webber: The Protestant Ethic and the Spirit of Capitalism*. New York: Charles Scribner's Sons.

Pavkov, T. W., and Pierce, K. A. 1999. *Ready, Set, Go: A Student Guide to SPSS 8.0 for Windows*.

Pelletier, E., and Evans, D. 2019. Beyond recidivism: Positive outcomes from higher education programs in prison. *Journal of Correctional Education* 70(2):49–68.

Pendleton, E. P. 1988. Student-centered instruction: A prison college model for building self-esteem. *Journal of Correctional Education* 39:82–84.

Petersilia, J. 2004. What works in prisoner reentry? Reviewing and questioning the evidence. *Federal Probation* 68(2). Retrieved June 13, 2012, from http://www.uscourts. gov/fedprob/September_2004/whatworks.html.

___________. 2003. Prisoner reentry and criminological knowledge. *The Criminologist* (March/April) 28:2–5.

___________. 2001. When prisoners return to the community: Political, economic, and social consequences. *Sentencing & Corrections* (November) 9:1–8.

Peterson, C., and Seligman, M.E.P. 2004. *Character Strengths and Virtues: A Handbook and Classification*. New York: Oxford University Press.

Philosophy: Lawrence Kohlberg's stages of moral development. https://handwiki.org/wiki/Philosophy:Lawrence-_Kohlberg%27s_stages-of_moral_development. Retrieved 2022.

Piquero, A. R. 2012. Obeying signals and predicting future offending. *Criminology & Public Policy* 11(1):51–60.

Pollock, J. M. 2005. *Prisons: Today and Tomorrow*. 2nd ed. Sudbury, MA: Jones & Bartlett.

Pompoco, A., Wooldredge, J., Lugo, M., Sullivan, C., and Latessa, E. 2017. Reducing inmate misconduct and prison return with facility education programs. *Criminology & Public Policy* 16:515–47.

Porporino, F. J., and Robinson, D. 1992. The correctional benefits of education: A follow-up of Canadian Federal Offenders participating in ABE. *Journal of Correctional Education* 43:92–98.

Pryor, M., and Thompkins, D. 2013. The disconnect between education and social opportunity for formerly incarcerated. *American Journal of Criminal Justice* 38: 457–79.

Quinney, R. 1970. *The Social Reality of Crime*. New York: Little, Brown.

RAND Corporation. 2019. Prison-based college presents challenges, but can succeed, study finds. Retrieved June 17, 2021 from https//phys.org/new/2019-05-prison-based-college.html.

Reagen, M. V., and Stoughton, D. M. 1976. *School Behind Bars: A Descriptive Overview of Correctional Education in the American Prison System*. Metuchen NJ: The Scarecrow.

Redondo, S., Sanchez-Mecca, J., and Garrido, V. 2002. "Crime Treatment in Europe: A Review of Outcome Studies." In *Offender Rehabilitation and Programmes and Policies to Reduce Re-offending*, edited by J. McGuire. New York: John Wiley.

Reiman, J. 2004. *The Rich Get Richer and the Poor Get Prison: Ideology, Class, and Criminal Justice*. 7th ed. Boston: Allyn & Bacon.

Reiman, J., and Leighton, P. 2017. *The Rich Get Richer and the Poor Get Prison: Ideology, Class, and Criminal Justice*. 11th ed. New York: Routledge.

Rentschler, W. H. 2001. "Lock Em Up and Throw Away the Key: A Policy That Won't Work." Annual Edition Corrections, pp.181–83.

Richards, S. T., and Jeffrey, I. R. 2001. Introducing the new school of convict criminology. *Social Justice* 28(1):177–90.

Roach, R. 2009. "Returning Home: Scholars Say More Research Is Needed on the Societal Reentry of the Formerly Incarcerated." In *Critical Issues in Criminal Justice*, 1st ed., edited by R. G. Burns. Upper Saddle River, NJ: Pearson/Prentice Hall.

Robinson, R. L., Jr. 1990. "The Relationship Between Recidivism of Missouri Parolees and Participation in an Associate Degree of Vocational Program." Unpublished dissertation, University of Missouri, Columbia.

Robinson, G., and English, E. 2017. *The Second Chance Pell Pilot Program: A Historical Overview*. American Enterprise Institute.

Ross, R. R. 1995. "The Reasoning and Rehabilitation Program for High-Risk Probationers and Prisoners." In *Going Straight: Effective Delinquency Prevention and Offender Rehabilitation*, edited by R. R. Ross, D. H. Antonowicz, and G. K. Dhaliwal. Ottawa, Canada: Air Training & Publications.

___________. 1985. *Time to Think: A Cognitive Model of Delinquency Prevention and Offender Rehabilitation*. Johnson City, TN:

Ross, R. R., Antonowicz, D. H., and Dhaliwal, G. K. 1995. *Going Straight: Effective Delinquency Prevention and Offender Rehabilitation*. Ottawa, Canada: Air Training & Publications.

Ross, R. R., and Fabiano, E. A.1983. *The Cognitive Model of Crime, and Delinquency Prevention and Rehabilitation: Intervention Techniques*. Ottawa, Canada: Ontario Ministry of Correctional Services.

Salekin, R. 2002. Psychopathy and therapeutic pessimism: Clinical lore or clinical reality? *Clinical Psychology Review* 22:79–112.

Samenow, S. E. 1991. Correctional errors of thinking in the socialization of offenders. *Journal of Correctional Education* 42:56–58.

Schnur, A. C. 1948. The educational treatment of prisoners and recidivism. *American Journal of Sociology* (September) 54:142–47.

Schriro, D. 2012. Good science, good sense: Making meaningful change happen: A practitioner perspective. *Criminology & Public Policy* 11(1):101–10.

Schumacker, R., Anderson, D. B., and Anderson, S. L. 1990. Vocational and academic indicators of parole success. *Journal of Correctional Education* 41:8–12.

Scott,. 2018. Reducing recidivism via college-in-prison thoughts on data collection, methodology, and the question of purpose. *Critical Education* 9(18):1–15.

Scott, W. R. 2002. *Organizations: Rational, Natural, and Open Systems*. Upper Saddle River, NJ: Prentice Hall.

Seashore, M. J. 1976. *Prison Education Project Newgate and Other College Programs*. Washington: Prager.

Shapiro, T. M. 1999. *Great Divides: Readings in Social Inequality in the United States*. Mountain View, CA: Mayfield.

Shelden, R. G. 2001. *Controlling the Dangerous Classes: A Critical Introduction to the History of Criminal Justice*. Boston: Allyn & Bacon

Simon, J. 1993. *Poor Discipline*. Chicago, IL.: University of Chicago Press.

Stanley, T. D., and Doucouliagos, C. H. 2014. Meta-regression approximations to reduce publication selection bias. *Research Synthesis Methods* 5(1):60–78.

State of New York Department of Correctional Services. 1989. "Follow-up Study of a Sample of Offenders who Earned High School Equivalency Diplomas While Incarcerated." Microfilmed for New York State Library, November, 1992.

Steurer, S., Linton, J., Nally, J., and Lockwood, S. 2010. The top nine reasons to increase correctional education programs. *Corrections Today* 40–43.

Steurer, S., Smith, L., and Tracy A. 2001. *The Three-State Recidivism Study*. Correctional Education Association.

Stevens, D. J., and Ward, C. S. 1997. College education and recidivism: Educating criminals is meritorious. *Journal of Correctional Education* 48:106–11.

Sullivan, L. E. 1990. *The Prison Reform Movement Forlorn Hope*. Boston: Twayne.

Sullivan, D., and Tifft, L. 2005. *Restorative Justice: Healing the Foundations of our Everyday Lives*. Monsey, NY: Willow Tree Press.

___________. 2005. *Restorative Justice: Healing the Foundations of Our Everyday Lives.* Monsey, NY: Willow Tree Press. Corrections, pp., 126–58. Englewood Cliffs, NJ: Prentice Hall.

Sweetland, S. R. 1996. Human capital theory: Foundations of a field of inquiry. *Review of Educational Research* 66:341–59.

Sykes, G. M. 1958. *The Society of Captives: A Study of a Maximum Security Prison.* Princeton, NJ: Princeton University Press.

Szifris, K. 2017. Socrates and Aristotle: The role of ancient philosophers in the self-understanding of desisting prisoners. *Howard Journal of Crime & Justice* 56(4): 419–36.

Taylor, J. M., and Tewksbury, R. 2002. "Postsecondary Correctional Education: The Imprisoned University." In *Turnstile justice: Issues in American corrections*, edited by T. Alleman and R. L. Gido, pp.126–58. Englewood Cliffs, NJ: Prentice Hall.

Tewksbury, R. 1994. Literacy programming for jail inmates: Reflections and recommendations from one program. *Prison Journal* 74:16–27.

Tewksbury, R., Erickson, D. J., and Taylor, J. M. 2000. Opportunity lost: The consequences of eliminating Pell Grant eligibility for correctional education students. *Journal of Offender Rehabilitation* 31:43–56.

Tewksbury, R., and Taylor, J. M. 1996. The consequences of eliminating Pell Grants eligibility for students in post-secondary correctional education programs. *Federal Probation* 60:60–63.

Tipton, E. 2015. Small sample adjustments for robust variance estimation with meta-regression. *Psychological Methods* 20(3):375–03.

Tootoonchi, A. 1990. College education in prison: The inmates' perspectives. *Federal Probation* (December):34–40.

Tracy, A., Smith, L. G., and Steurer, S. 1998. Standing up for education. *Corrections Today* (April):144–56.

Travis, J. 2009a. *But They All Come Back: Facing the Challenges of Prisoner Reentry*. Washington, DC: Urban Institute Press.

___________. 2009b. "What Works for Successful Prisoner Reentry." Paper presented at the House of Representatives Appropriates Subcommittee on Commerce, Justice, Sciences and Related Agencies. Washington, DC. Retrieved June 13, 2012, from jjay.cuny.edu/Travis_Congre–ssional_Testimony.pdf.

Turk, A. 1966. Conflict and criminality. *American Sociological Review* 31:338–52.

Turker, W. 1999. "Unbroken Window." In *Annual Editions: Urban Society* by F. Siegel and J. Rosenberg, pp. 186–88. Dushkin/McGraw Hill.

Ubah, C. B. A. 2014. Using recidivism rate as the sole indicator of prison-based rehabilitation program usefulness: Lessons for 21st century corrections policy. *Journal of Social Science for Policy Implications* 2(1):67–83.

___________. 2005. An examination of academic, policy and social considerations of correctional education and offender recidivism: Lessons for 21st century criminology. *Justice Policy Journal* 2(2):1–17.

___________. 2003. Reaffirming the limits of offender rehabilitation but with caution. *A Critical Journal of Crime, Law, and Society* 16(3):197–203.

___________. 2002. A critical examination of empirical studies of offender rehabilitation-correctional education: Lessons for the 21st century. *Journal of Correctional Education* 53(1):13–19.

___________. 2001. "Correctional Education and Offender Recidivism: A Study of the Elimination of Pell Grants for Correctional Education Programs." Unpublished dissertation, Southern Illinois University, Carbondale.

Ubah, C. B. A., and Robinson, R. L. 2002. A grounded look at the debate over prison-based education: Optimistic theory versus pessimistic worldview. *The Prison Journal* 83:155–29.

Ubah, C. B. A., and Ubah, P. N. 2019. Individual change perspectives of offender rehabilitation: A narrative of their strengths. *The Pursuit* 2(2):29–56.

United Nations. 1948. "Universal Declaration of Human Rights," Article 26. Paris: United Nations.

United Nations. 1955. "Standard Minimum Rules for Treatment of Offenders." Congress on the Prevention of Crime and Treatment of Offenders, Geneva, Switzerland.

United States Government Accountability Office. 2019. "Federal Student Aid: Actions Needed to Evaluate Pell Grant Pilot for Incarcerated Students." United States Government Accountability Office, pp. 1–54.

United States Sentencing Commission. 2016. "Recidivism among Federal Offenders: A Comprehensive Overview." www.ussc.gov.

Vandala, N. G. 2019. The transformative effect of correctional education: A global perspective. *Cogent Social Sciences* 5(1):1–35. https://doi.org/10.1080/23311886.2019.1677122.

Veysey, B. M. 2008. Rethinking reentry. *The Criminologist* (May/June) 33(3):2–5.

Vinney, C. 2019. Kohlberg's stages of moral development. https://www.thoughtco.com/kohlbergs-stages-of-moral-development-4689125.

Visher, C. A., Debus-Sherrill, S. A., and Yahner, J. 2011. Employment after prison: A longitudinal study of former prisoners. *Justice Quarterly* 28:698–718.

Wade, D. T., and de Jong, B. A. 2000. Recent advances in rehabilitation. *British Medical Journal* 320:1385–88.

Walker, S., Spohn, C., and Delone, M. 2000. *Race, Ethnicity, and Crime in America: The Color of Justice*. 2nd ed. Australia: Wadsworth Thomson Learning.

Wang, X., Mears, D. P., and Bales, W. D. 2010. Race-specific employment contexts and recidivism. *Criminology* 48(4):1171–211.

Ward, T., and Maruna, S. 2007. *Rehabilitation: Beyond the Risk Paradigm*. New York: Routledge.

Ward, T., and Stewart, C. 2003. Criminogenic needs and human needs: A theoretical model. *Psychology, Crime & Law* 9:125–43.

Weir, J. D. 1973. "A History of Education in Canadian Federal Correction." In *Readings in Prison Education*, edited by A. R. Roberts, pp. 39–47. Springfield: Charles C. Thomas.

Weisburd, D., Farrington, D. P., and Gill, C. 2017. What works in crime prevention and rehabilitation: An assessment of systematic reviews. *Criminology & Public Policy* 16(2):415–49.

Welch, M. 2004. *Corrections: A Critical Approach*. 2nd ed. Boston: McGraw Hill.

___________. 1996. *Corrections: A Critical Approach*. New York: McGraw Hill.

Wheeler, D. P., and Patterson, G. 2008. Prisoner reentry. *Health & Social Work* 33:145–47.

White, V., Applegarth, D. M., Hunt, J., and Hudgins, C. 2022. "The NIJ Recidivism Forecasting Challenge: Contextualizing the Results." National Institute of Justice/NIJ.OJP.GOV.

Wilkinson, R., and Pickett, K. 2010. *The Spirit Level: Why Greater Equality Makes Societies Stronger*. New York: Bloomsbury Press.

Williams, F. P., 3rd, and McShane, M. D. 2014. *Criminological Theory*. 6th ed. Boston: Pearson.

Wilson, J. 2005. Bad behavior or bad policy? An examination of Tennessee release cohorts, 1993–2001. *Criminology & Public Policy* 4(3):485–518.

Wilson, J. A. 2011. What did we learn from the evaluation of project greenlight? *Federal Sentencing Reporter* 24(1):76–79.

Wilson, P. R. 1994. Recidivism and vocational education. *Journal of Correctional Education* 45:158–63.

Wilson, D. B., Gallagher, C. A., and Mackenzie, D. L. (2000). A meta-analysis of corrections-based education, vocation, and work programs for adult offenders. *Journal of Research in Crime & Delinquency* 37(4):347–68.

Wilson, J. Q., and Kelling, G. L. 1999. "Broken Windows." In *Annual Edition: Urban Society*, edited by F. Siegel and J. Rosenberg, pp.178–85. Dushkin/McGraw Hill.

Wood, R. L. 1997. "An Analysis of Crucial U.S. Education Legislation: 1940–1996." www.ocpathink.org/education/edleg.htm. March, pp. 1–20.

Wormith, J. S., Althouse, R., Simpson, M. Reitzel, L. R., Fagan, T. J., and Morgan, R. D. 2007. The rehabilitation and reintegration of offenders: The current landscape and some future directions for correctional psychology. *Criminal Justice & Behavior* 34:179–92.

Yates, M. T. 2012. *Prisoner Education Debates in Congress: Elite Discourse and Policymaking*. El Paso, TX: LFB Scholarly Publishing.

Zink, T. M. 1970. A study of the effect of prison education on societal adjustment. *Journal of Correctional Education* 22:18–20.

Zook, J. 1994. Ban on Pell Grants to inmates crushes prison-education efforts. *Chronicle of Higher Education* (November) 9:32–34.

Zucker, L. G. 1987. Institutional theories of organization. *Annual Review of Sociology* 13:443–64.

About the Author

Charles B. A. Ubah, PhD is a professor of Criminology, Criminal Justice, Law, Sociology, and Public Policy at Georgia College & State University-Milledgeville. Dr. Ubah has published manuscripts in a variety of peer-reviewed journals and books in the areas of his interest and focus, which include criminology, criminal justice, law, sociology, and public policy. He has been active in the American Society of Criminology, Academy of Criminal Justice Sciences, Southern Criminal Justice Association, Criminal Justice Association of Georgia, the African Criminology and Justice Association, and the University System of Georgia Africa Council. He obtained a Doctoral Degree (PhD) in Criminology/Sociology from Southern Illinois University, Carbondale, Illinois; Master of Arts and Bachelor of Science (Honors) in Criminal Justice/Sociology from Lincoln University, Jefferson City, Missouri. He has held various administrative positions in different capacities in the academy. Currently he serves as chair of the University System of Georgia Africa Council (a consortium of 26 public universities and colleges, including some private institutions).

Address correspondence to Dr. Charles B. A. Ubah, Department of Government and Sociology, Georgia College & State University, Campus Box 18, Milledgeville, Georgia 31061–0490 (E-mail: Charles.ubah@gcsu.edu).

Index

www.ingramcontent.com/pod-product-compliance
Ingram Content Group UK Ltd.
Pitfield, Milton Keynes, MK11 3LW, UK
UKHW041839031026
15587UKWH00002B/885

9 781666 922790